Tacita Dean

Woman with a Red Hat

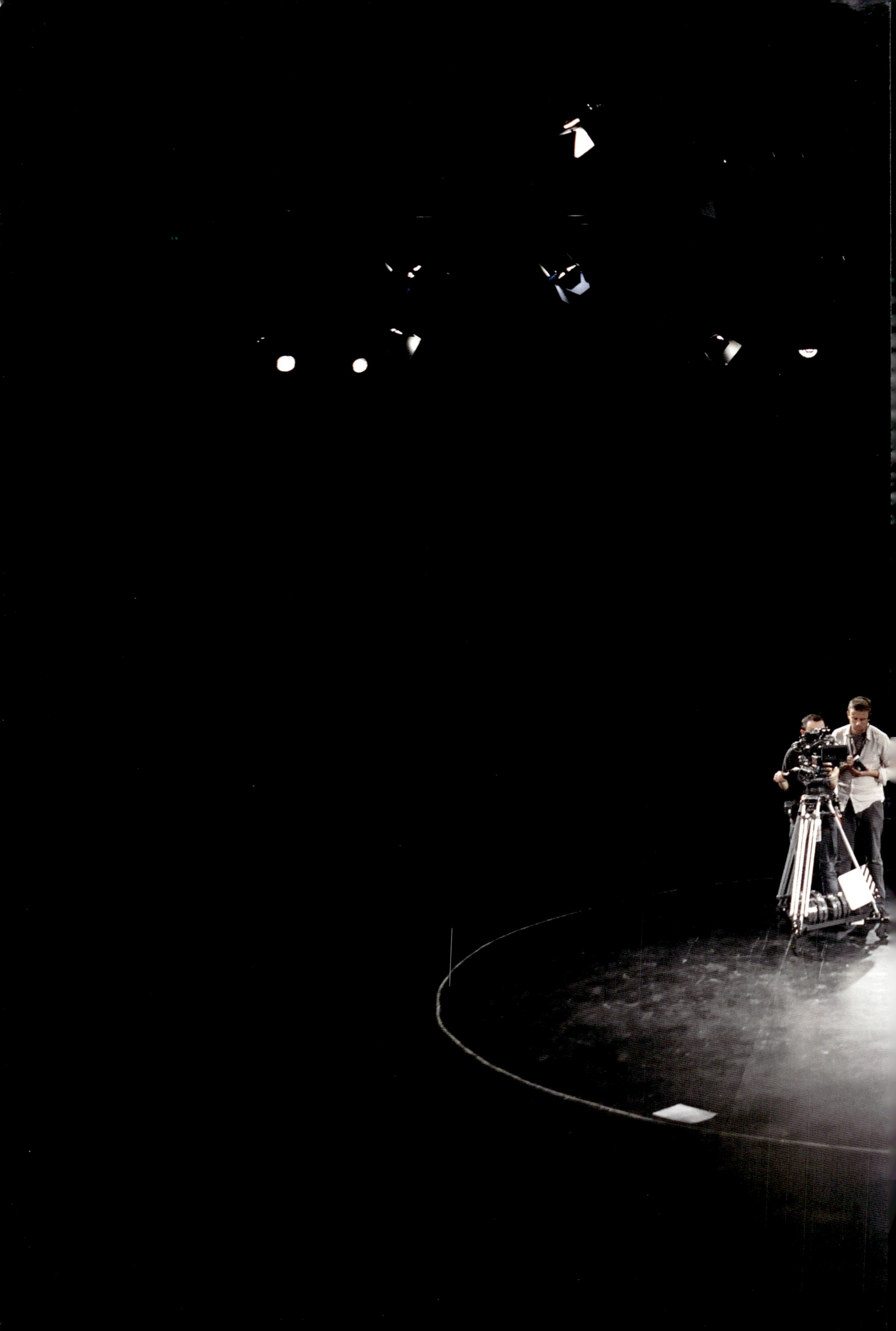

Tacita Dean

Woman with a Red Hat

This exhibition represents the material breadth of the work of British-European artist Tacita Dean (b.1965, Canterbury) – from drawing and print-making, to film and installation – yet at the same time it is highly focused in its thematic approach. *Woman with a Red Hat* is concerned with theatre, performance and the figure of the actor in Dean's work. Through work made from 1996 to the present day, it examines the way in which narratives are constructed both on stage and screen.

The exhibition is centred on ***Event for a Stage*** (50 mins, 2015), shown in the upper gallery (see reverse for screening times). In this film, actor Stephen Dillane tests and troubles over the artifice of theatre and the role of the script, describing the collective effort of performer and audience that creates 'the magic of suspended disbelief that is theatre'. Using pages of script handed to him by Dean, the actor steps from narrative readings and apparently autobiographical stories to recitations from Shakespeare's *The Tempest*. The line between reality and fiction is blurred as Dillane moves from one voice to another, alternately playing 'himself' and the 'actor' as a type. As the piece

Continues until 30 Sep 2018
Festival opening hours, 10am–7pm
Free entry

The Fruitmarket Gallery
45 Market Street, Edinburgh EH1 1DF
P +44 (0)131 225 2383
E info@fruitmarket.co.uk

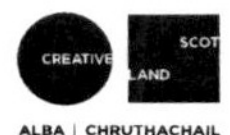

unfolds, the 'woman with a red hat' becomes a point of focus for the actor's self-consciousness on the one hand, and his self-assuredness on the other.

The lines that open *Event for a Stage* – 'Storm, storm, storm' – reverberate through the imagery of the monumental blackboard drawing, ***When first I raised the Tempest*** (2016), whose skies seem to shift and billow as the natural light moves over them. Emerging from the storm clouds are handwritten words and phrases recalling lines and characters from *The Tempest*, like a partial, fragmented script.

Two other films are shown upstairs: ***His Picture in Little*** (15 1/2 mins, 2017) and ***Providence*** (5 1/2 mins, 2017). Both on 16mm celluloid, the films are back-projected onto screens made of stretched vinyl, a delicate membrane through which the light of the projector shines from a hidden booth. *His Picture in Little* takes its title from a line in Act II Scene II of *Hamlet*, describing a portrait miniature. Dean's film follows the conventions of miniature portraiture and depicts three actors who have all played Hamlet on the London stage – David Warner, Stephen Dillane and Ben Whishaw – each of a different generation. The film uses a technique developed by Dean in which she exposes the negative multiple times, masking a different section on each successive exposure, and so creating chance juxtapositions between the actors. In *Providence*, this technique gives rise to an evocation of David Warner's reveries as he sits contemplatively, apparently conjuring up a hummingbird. In contrast to *Event for a Stage*, these short films show the actor at rest, between the moments in which he is alert to and self-conscious of the gaze of an audience.

Like these films, ***Die Regimentstochter*** (2005), named after a Donizetti opera, also foregrounds chance juxtapositions. This work arose when Dean found a collection of German opera programmes dating from the 1930s and '40s in a Berlin flea market. They were all mysteriously defaced by their former owner, with sections removed from their covers in what Dean saw as 'found collages', subsequently realising what had been cut out. In the first iteration of this work, Dean's only intervention was to frame the programmes: here they are shown in facsimile as an artist's book. The cut out sections act as performers of sound production in film – the foley artists – and the mechanisms by which sound is scripted, recorded, stored and played back. What it is missing is the visual of the film itself: the narrative of this imagined short film is told purely through scripted sound (voices, footsteps, closing doors, the wind). An usherette leaves a theatre just as actor Tim Pigott-Smith strikes up with the opening lines of *Henry IV Part II*, 'Open your ears'. Walking and running through various environments, she returns to the theatre for the last lines of the play. She is at the peripheries of the drama, like the foley artists, not centre-stage, but important nevertheless. As with many of the works in this exhibition, *Foley Artist* lays bare the artifice of performance, whilst at the same time conjuring its magic.

Screenings of *Event for a Stage* are free.
The film lasts 50 minutes and will be shown at the following times:
10.30am, 12 noon, 1.30pm, 3pm, 4.30pm, 5.45pm
Book via Eventbrite (bit.ly/Tacitadean) or in the bookshop, or speak to an Information Assistant about availability for the next showing.

For every exhibition, we organise a wide variety of events that offer you the chance to get closer to the art we show.
A portable FM hearing loop is available for all events.

All our talks and workshops are free so early booking is advised to guarantee your place. Book via Eventbrite, or phone 0131 226 8181.

Keep up to date with all our news and events
join our **e-bulletin** mailing list at **fruitmarket.co.uk**

The
Fruitmarket
Gallery

twitter @fruitmarket
facebook fruitmarketgallery
instagram @fruitmarketgallery

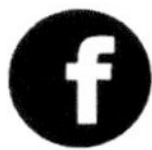

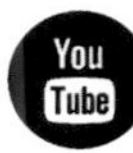

#tacitadean #fruitmarketgallery

The Fruitmarket Gallery is a company limited by guarantee, registered in Scotland No. 87888 and registered as a **Scottish Charity No. SC 005576**.
VAT No. 398 2504 21. Registered Office: 45 Market St, Edinburgh, EH1 1DF

windows onto photographs or texts, creating haunting fragmented portraits of opera singers and the narratives in which they performed.

Downstairs, another facet of the acting profession becomes evident in the sixteen ***Found Postcard Monoprints (Actors)*** (2018). These early twentieth-century postcards from the artist's collection of found postcards, range from unknown actors to the stars of their day – Buster Keaton, Sarah Bernhardt and Rudolph Valentino among them. These images show the posturing of the actor, ready for public consumption, but now partially obscured, or perhaps embellished, by the monoprinting process. This 'blind' printing technique – in which the artist creates marks without knowing exactly where they will print – makes for incidental alignments between ink and image.

Such coincidence also structures the short narrative of the film ***A Muse*** (2 1/2 mins, 2017), which uses the masking technique described above, staging a chance interaction between Ben Whishaw (who was in London) and poet, essayist and classicist Anne Carson and her partner Robert Currie (who were in Illinois). Whishaw appears to shout down to Carson, as she and Currie spin on a children's roundabout. This shared moment, in which each protagonist is 'a muse' for the other, is at once playfully natural and also entirely artificial, a conceit of the filming technique.

A more subdued tone is struck in the twenty photogravures which make up ***The Russian Ending*** (2001), which come from postcards collected by the artist from European flea markets. The handwritten notes that cover their surfaces read like snippets of scripts and film directions. Depicting disastrous and sombre scenes, from explosions to funerals, these images act as stand-ins for the final frames of imagined films. Drawing upon a convention of the Danish film industry, to produce films with two endings – a happy one for the American market, and a tragic one for the Russian market – Dean presents a series of disastrous 'Russian endings'. The part stands in for the whole, the apparent final frame invoking the events that might have led up to it.

Likewise, in ***Foley Artist*** (1996), parts indicate the whole, with sound pointing to an entire narrative. The installation reveals the hidden

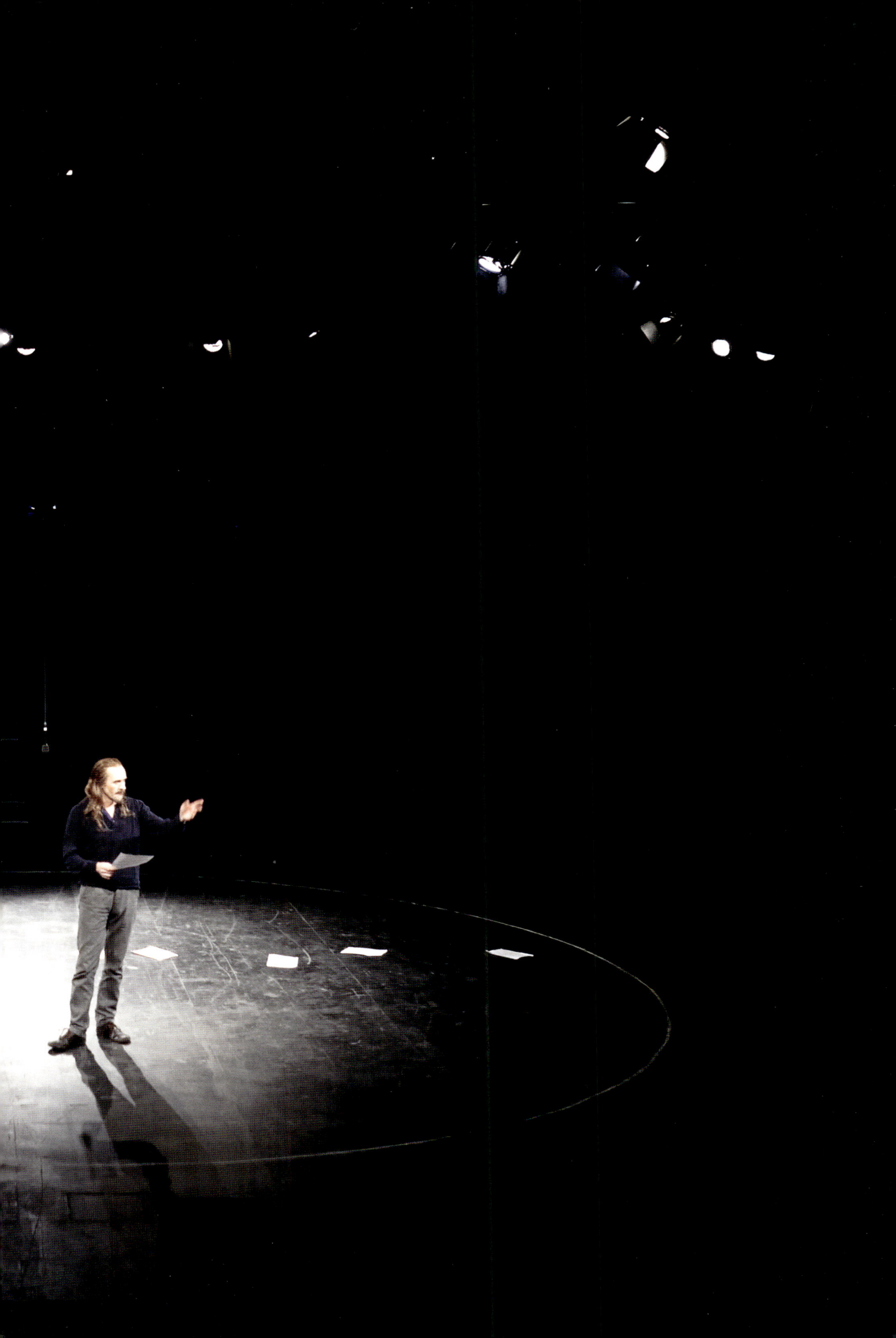

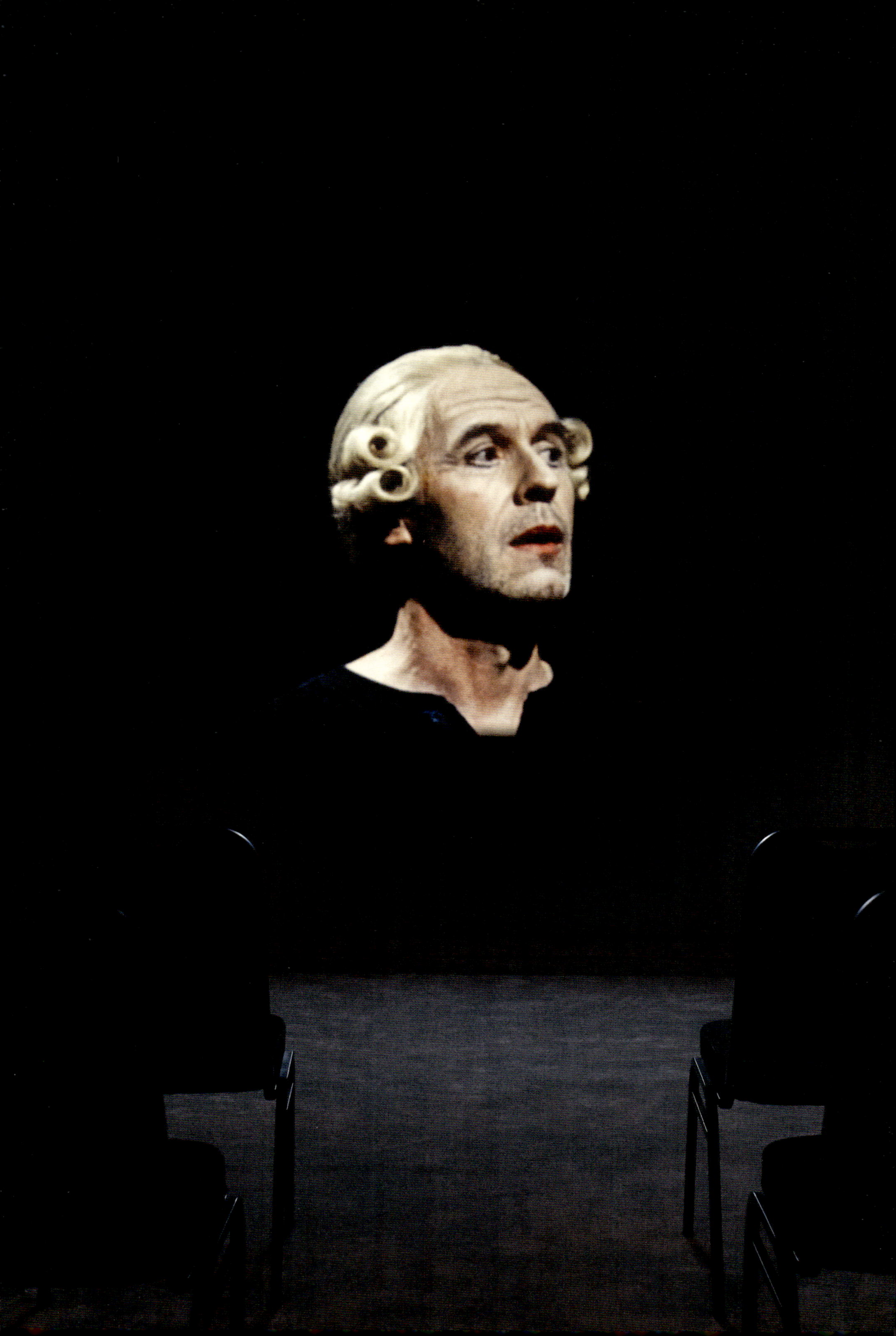

Event for a Stage

Camera A is inside the circle. Camera B is outside the circle.
Cameras start rolling as the audience enters.
The actor roams around inside the circle looking out.
The doors close and the audience quietens.

(clapper)

ACTOR

Camera B. Roll 1. End board.

(enters the circle)

Storm, storm, storm with people who you don't even know who they are and then a girl runs on and says: 'Father, did you do this?' So we know I'm her father and she's upset so I say 'Be collected' and then I tell her – and through her the audience why we're on this island and why I've created this storm.

Except I say it in words that are more or less incomprehensible.

Being once perfected how to grant suits,
How to deny them, who to advance and who
To trash for over-topping, new created
Those creatures that were mine, I say, or changed 'em,
Or else new form'd 'em; having both the key
Of officer and office, set all hearts i'the state
To what tune pleased his ear; that now he was
The ivy which had hid my princely trunk…

(actor leaves circle and looks straight out)

My mother loved the theatre when she was in her right mind. She may still love it now that she isn't, but she hasn't been for a while. I don't know how she'd know that she was watching theatre and not just 'life'.

(actor moves clockwise around the outside of the circle)

The first indication that we had that my father was losing his mind came when he created an unconventional relationship with the characters in a TV series.

(actor takes page of script from artist and enters circle)

ACTOR

The artist told me she has filmed people before – subjects, personages, but this time she is trying to film a process, a craft, a profession. She is interested in what she calls 'self-consciousness'. It is something she doesn't like to see in her films, she says, her subjects being 'aware' of themselves, aware of themselves being watched. She knew that actors, by definition, are always aware of themselves being watched. But are they ever not self-conscious?

(actor drops page of script to the floor and moves centre circle to the hanging microphone. He takes a torch, his glasses and a book from his pocket. Turns on torch and begins reading)

ACTOR

'One evening in the winter of 1801 I met an old friend in a public park. He had recently been appointed principal dancer at the local theatre. I told him I had been surprised to see him more than once at the marionette theatre which had been put up in the marketplace. He assured me that the mute gestures of these puppets gave him much satisfaction and told me bluntly that any dancer who wished to perfect his art could learn a lot from them. He asked me if I hadn't in fact found some of the dance movements of the puppets very graceful. This I couldn't deny. I inquired about the mechanism of these figures. I wanted to know how it is possible, without having a maze of strings attached to one's fingers, to move the separate limbs and extremities in the rhythm of the dance. His answer was that I must not imagine each limb as being individually positioned and moved by the operator in the various phases of the dance. Each movement, he told me, has its centre of gravity; it is enough to control this within the puppet. The limbs, which are only pendulums, then follow mechanically of their own accord, without further help. He added that this movement is very simple. When the centre of gravity is moved in a straight line, the limbs describe curves. Often shaken in a purely haphazard way, the puppet falls into a kind of rhythmic movement which resembles dance.'

(clapper)

Camera A. Roll 1. End board.

'This observation seemed to me to throw some light at last on the enjoyment he said he got from the marionette theatre, but I was far from guessing the inferences he would draw from it later.'

(closes book, turns off torch, takes off his glasses and puts everything away in his pocket. He then exits circle and starts walking anti-clockwise)

ACTOR

When I was a boy there were two types of magazine lying around the house: there were my mother's theatre magazines, which had black and white photographs of actors in plays, with make-up and costumes on stages with sets. They had the feeling of bodies in motion.

And there were my father's medical magazines, which had colour photographs of bodies, naked bodies and body parts and these were static, because they were illustrating a condition, often a skin condition, or a deformity, and often because they were dead.

(takes page of script from artist and enters circle)

ACTOR

She said have you ever had stage fright? No. What do you mean by stage fright? Have I ever forgotten my words? Have I ever dried?

(drops page of script)

Being once perfected how to grant suits,
How to deny them, who to advance and who
To trash for over-topping, new created
Those creatures that were mine, I say, or changed 'em
Or else new form'd 'em; having both the key

Of officer and office, set all hearts i'the state
To what tune pleased his ear; that now he was
The ivy which had hid my princely trunk...

(exits circle in direction of artist)

ACTOR

*My father was from the Blue Mountains. He died just before Christmas.
We scattered his ashes up there last week.*

(picks up page of script from artist and enters circle)

ACTOR

This is a stage. The stage is my habitat; where I have been trained to be at ease.

(walks to inside edge of circle looking out)

There is an invisible thing around this stage, separating me from you: you, being the audience. It is a film of protection; it protects me, and the action on stage, and it also protects you. Above all, it protects the magic of suspended disbelief that is theatre. Without the invisible film that contains everything on the stage there would be no context for my actions, no discourse, no history.

(starts to move anti-clockwise)

This invisible thing – like a membrane perhaps, or more like connective tissue – is what makes theatre theatre. Without the separation the spectacle would become life. Theatre is life as spectacle. Theatre is what makes life more interesting than theatre.

Art is what makes life more interesting than art.

(drops page of script, exits circle and starts walking anti-clockwise)

ACTOR

When we cremated him on a cold wet dark grey day in Brighton, England, we stuck photographs of him on the side of the bright yellow cardboard coffin. Most of these were black and white photographs of him as a boy in the bush and one under a jacaranda tree at Sydney University where he graduated in 1952... All the talk at the funeral was of his Australianness although he'd spent 25 years in Australia and more than twice that in England.

(clapper)

Camera B. Roll 2. End board.

(continues walking)

When he was in the nursing home and still capable of resistance he'd sometimes lie on the floor at bedtime so the nurses couldn't get him up and they had to cover him where he lay and he'd say 'I'm off camping in the mountains.'

(turns and retraces his steps)

I don't know why, if he loved Australia so much, he left it but – for the sake of the story (and everything I say is for the sake of the story) let's say he did.

(takes page of script and enters circle)

ACTOR

Sometimes this membrane between us, which makes you the audience and me the actor, gets ruptured. I don't mean an artistic rupture – the deliberate transgressing of the thing, which divides us in order to find a different or deeper connection between us – I mean an actual rupture. A hole broken through it. When that happens, a spell is broken. Our confidence in the artifice is shattered and it can feel dangerous.

The audience's experience of the membrane is that it holds, by and large, it contains; it's flexible. The audience feels pretty safe to experience whatever it's experiencing and doesn't notice the things that the actor notices, which threaten to puncture the membrane. In this way actors are like good parents, protecting the audience's fragile belief. But also, like parents, desperately trying to maintain the illusion of their own belief.

If the actor is unable or unwilling to maintain the integrity of the membrane, real life enters the space. The audience take a while to wake up to it but when they do… they see…

(drops script, exits circle and stands facing in)

ACTOR

…Hitch hiking in the south of France aged 16, with a friend, we were standing on a slip road outside Marseilles looking down on the traffic rushing past on the autoroute about 100 yards below. It was very, very hot; we were sunburnt; we were tired and bored. We'd been waiting a long time and it took us a while to realise that something was happening which wasn't what we expected. There was a car, a small car rolling over and over on its roof down the middle lane like tumbleweed. We watched as it rolled and rolled while the other cars carried on behaving as cars do and then it smashed into the base of one of the big iron stanchions that hold up the autoroute signs.

(walks around circle clockwise to pick up page of script. Enters circle)

ACTOR

I am an actor playing the role of an actor on this stage. Unfortunately 'the actor' is no role at all. She – the artist – asked me to play the role of an actor, the role of the actor being filmed on stage. She said she wanted to make a portrait of an actor in context, in his natural habitat, like a beast in its lair.

I said I don't really do stage acting anymore.

'Don't you?' she said. 'Well, why did you agree to come?'

(keeps page of script, steps out of circle walking clockwise)

ACTOR

Once at dinner my father said, 'Why don't you be an actor, that's useful?'

(steps into circle then out again)

He was getting at my mother.

(enters circle)

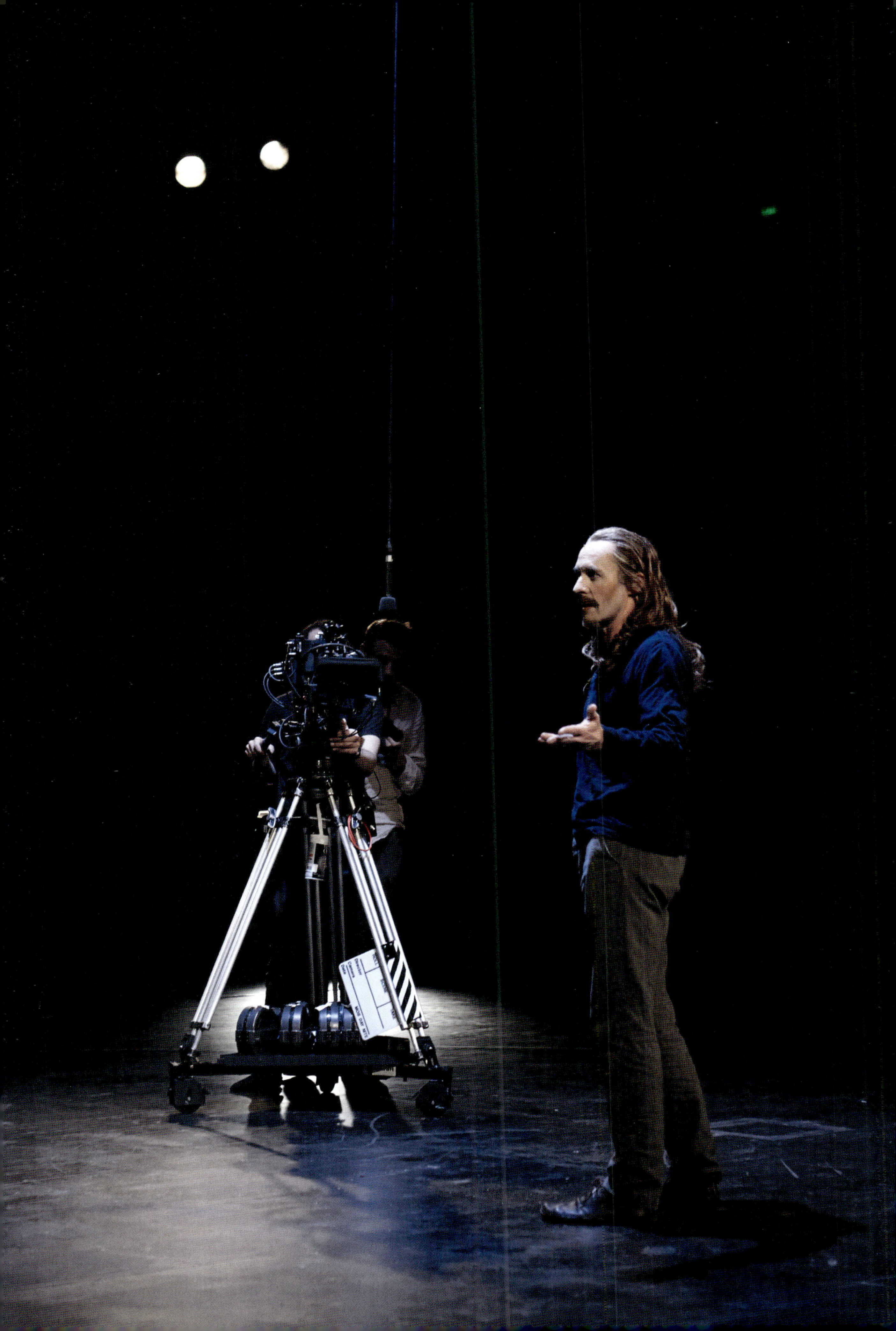

ACTOR

When I was asked if I wanted to come and play the role of an actor on stage I said no. I said, 'Will there be a text?' She said, 'I don't know.' I said, 'That's quite a risk. How long would I be on stage?'

'About forty minutes, I think.' 'That's quite a long time to be on stage alone.' She said, 'Is it?' I said I could imagine taking such a risk in Paris or Berlin but I didn't think I'd want to go to the other side of the world to do something I don't know what it is.

(drops page of script and exits circle walking clockwise)

ACTOR

Since my father died, I've had two dreams about trying to get to the Australian embassy. Not the actual embassy in London on the Strand where I go to get my passport renewed: the idea of an embassy in dreamspace. In one of the dreams, there's a kangaroo standing in front of a gate, and I understood this kangaroo to have a great capacity for violence: a sort of a bouncer. I knew I'd have to show…

(clapper)

Camera A. Roll 2. End board.

…great physical courage to get through.

(pauses)

Years ago, when I left school I was thinking of coming to college in Australia but my father said I wouldn't get a passport so I didn't pursue it.

(picks up pages of script)

ACTOR

An actor is the highest form of life. The job is to embody text in a believable way for an audience. The more diverse texts you can skilfully embody, the more of an actor or player you are. Everybody is embodying a text in their life. The origin of the text is mysterious with a capital M but it has been said by Montaigne that a good life is a life well played. In other words, whichever text or texts you have chosen to play out, or which have chosen you, you embody as convincingly or as fully as you can before you die knowing that you are simply an instrument for the music, for the text to play. The actor, though, because he moves lightly between lots of texts not only has a privileged insight into the provisionality of all texts but he has had to develop the capacity to inhabit the space between texts; a place of compromised identity, where there may be no language.

When we are confident in our text, we are undivided, no longer alienated from language.

(exits circle putting script pages down.
Stands speaking across circle)

ACTOR

Sometimes I talk to my mother about a play or a film that I've watched, which I know she can't possibly have seen or know anything about, and she'll say something like 'Yes, I did see that but I felt people really weren't taking it on board and they felt hungry.'

She's able to imitate the patterns and tropes and rhythms of conversation without the slightest need to know anything about what she's talking about. And she enjoys it – she feels no need to know more than she does.

When she sits with the other people in the nursing home and they all chat together, their conversation disappears into the air like loose threads blowing in the wind.

(picks up script pages and enters circle)

ACTOR

The artist sent me a script. I told her, 'Why don't you get an actor to do this?' She said, 'I thought I had.'

I told her that her text didn't sound like me: 'I wouldn't say things in that way.' She said, 'Well, it's not supposed to be you; it's supposed to be "the actor". That's the point: it's artifice – a remove – transformation.'

I rewrote it.

'Another thing,' I said, 'The main reason I always chose or didn't choose to do a piece of theatre was the quality of the text. People choose to work with all sorts of texts but I have really only worked with "great" ones. A great text is the means by which I get through the time and space on the stage. I can trust it with my life.

That means that I am actually only present in the time and space through the agency of the text.

And this is not a great text. I don't know what this is. I don't know what this is.'

(clapper)

Camera B. Roll 3. End board.

When I was confident on stage I was freer than anywhere else. I knew the past and the future and I was wholly present to myself, to everyone else on the stage, to my imagination, to the audience and to the entire environment – the reality being created on stage and the fire exit and the fire exit and the lady in the red hat and the noise of the traffic outside. Present to everything. That's when you're really flying.

'And when you're not confident?' she said.

It's a struggle to get from second to second. Intense self-consciousness. I force my way through it, lurching. I try to take myself by surprise so sometimes I turn upstage and just pull a stupid face, just to generate some energy but then I know I'm trying too hard and I feel it must be obvious to the imaginary splintered off part of myself sitting in the audience who's judging me, angry that I'm giving one of those awful overwrought, overworked performances that make you despise actors and the theatre and why you never go any more. Fear, humiliation and I wish I could leave the stage.

(drops script pages and leaves theatre banging fire exit door)

(await his return)

(returns by different fire exit entering circle)

'I pray thee, mark me.'

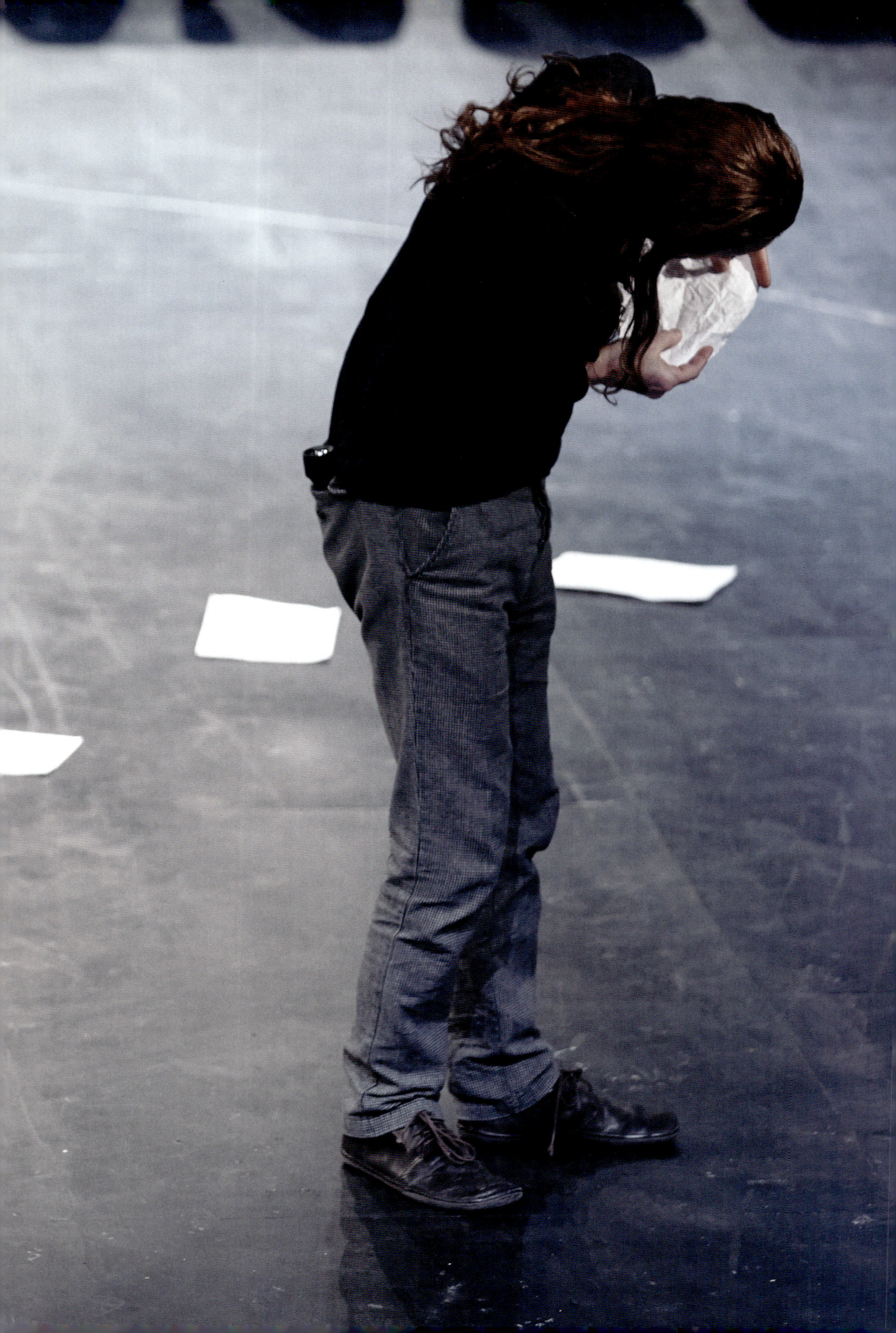

(looks for correct script pages)

'Have you ever had stage fright?'

(drops script pages)

'I, thus neglecting worldly ends, all dedicated
To closeness and the bettering of my mind...

(clapper)

Camera A. Roll 3. End board.

...in my false brother
Awaked an evil nature; and my trust,
Like a good parent, did beget of him
A falsehood in its contrary as great
As my trust was; which had indeed no limit,
A confidence sans bound. He being thus perfected...

(silence)

To have no screen between the part he play'd
And him he play'd it for, he needs will be
Absolute Milan. Me poor man, my library
Was dukedom large enough; confederates –
So dry he was...'

(silence)

ARTIST

(unmic'ed)

God that must be awful.

ACTOR

What?

(exits circle towards artist, picks up page of script and re-enters circle)

'God that must have been awful,' she said.

I looked out at the audience and I could see these important people looking at me looking at them – it was a big opening night in New York – and I could see the fire exit signs and the lady in the red hat, and the handbags in the aisles. I turned upstage and looked offstage into the empty open wings where I'd been waiting to come on a few moments before and I thought I could just leave.

It wasn't awful – it was better than carrying on.

She said: 'Fire exit, fire exit, woman with a red hat: but your description of the two moments is the same? Flying and drying? Are they the extremes of self-consciousness? In one you are in a perfect equilibrium with your presence on stage and the audience and the text, but in the other you are lost and beyond self-awareness, and the connective tissue has broken down.

Is that what happened? Did you want to destroy the membrane? Is that why you've stopped acting?'

(drops script page in circle and exits circle, walking clockwise twice around the circumference of circle getting slower and slower)

ACTOR

I came to Australia in the year before my brother died to make a TV series in the outback. While I was there, I met a lot of old fellas out there who reminded me of my dad, just the way they were, the way they talked – the stories they told and the way they told them, dragging them out, taking time over every word, 'cos it was so bloody hot.

(exits circle towards artist, picks up page of script and re-enters circle)

ACTOR

What is stage fright? The inability to step on stage? Disenchantment. DIS-EN-CHANT-MENT. Dis-en-chantment. Have I got it now? Is that why I stopped?

(screws up the page of script into a ball, squeezing it hard)

(clapper)

Camera B. Roll 4. End board.

An actor is the lowest form of life. I have no will of my own.

(throws script back into circle as he exits. Stands outside looking back in)

ACTOR

My mother's dementia is more benign, apparently at least, than my father's was. Sometimes I had the feeling with him that he was terrifyingly aware of the mental and physical prison that he was in. My mother is in a kind of bliss. When we walk in the garden of the nursing home she'll always point out the same avenue of trees and say how much she loves them as if she's never seen them before. And then five minutes later she says the same thing again. Last time I was there she said she loved them so much she thought she could live there, and I said, well that's lucky because you do and she said, 'Yes and they make you feel as if you belong so you know which ones will come down and which ones will stay.'

And then we went round the other side and we sat on a bench and looked out over the fields in the sunshine and she looked up and she said, 'This is just perfect. Those big things up there with status and they don't move – and they don't need to move!' 'And,' (delightedly indicating the air), 'Look at all the leaves, no not leaves. I feel them all around me and there's a big white one coming up behind me.'

(walks clockwise to pick up page of script and enters the circle)

ACTOR

In rehearsal I use the text to weave a more or less complex pattern of threads of emotional and imaginative connection into something like a rope which I then use with my eyes open in the rehearsal room until I am so familiar with it that I use it with my eyes closed, which is a performance. Then memory, imagination, language and utterance are one thing and are embodied. And in the second performance I've forgotten it all and start again as if it had never happened before.

(drops page of script and takes book and glasses out of his pocket,
moving to the hanging microphone at centre of circle)

ACTOR

'In this connection,' said my friend warmly, 'I must tell you another story. You'll easily see how it fits in here.

When I was on my way to Russia, I spent some time on the estate of a Baltic nobleman whose sons had a passion for fencing. The elder, in particular, who had just come down from the university, thought he was a bit of an expert. One morning, when I was in his room, he offered me a rapier. I accepted his challenge but, as it turned out, I had the better of him. It made him angry, and this increased his confusion. Nearly every thrust I made found its mark. At last his rapier flew into the corner of the room. As he picked it up he said, half in anger and half in jest, that he had met his master but that there is a master for everyone and everything – and now he proposed to lead me to mine. The brothers laughed loudly at this and shouted: 'Come on, down to the shed!' They took me by the hand and led me outside to make the acquaintance of a bear which their father was rearing on the farm.

I was astounded to see the bear standing upright on his hind legs, his back against the post to which he was chained, his right paw raised ready for battle. He looked me straight in the eye. This was his fighting posture. I wasn't sure if I was dreaming, seeing such an opponent. They urged me to attack. 'See if you can hit him!' they shouted. As I had now recovered somewhat from my astonishment I fell on him with my rapier. The bear made a slight movement with his paw and parried my thrust. I feinted to deceive him. The bear did not move. I attacked again, this time with all the skill I could muster. I know I would certainly have thrust my way through to a human breast, but the bear made a slight movement with its paw and parried my thrust. By now I was almost in the same state as the elder brother had been: the bear's utter seriousness robbed me of my composure. Thrusts and feints followed…

(clapper)

Camera A. Roll 4. End board.

…thick and fast, the sweat poured off me, but in vain. It wasn't merely that he parried my thrusts like the finest fencer in the world; when I feinted to deceive him he made no move at all. No human fencer could equal his perception in this respect. He stood upright, his paw raised ready for battle, his eye fixed on mine as if he could read my soul there, and when my thrusts were not meant seriously he did not move. Do you believe this story?'

'Absolutely,' I said with joyful approval. 'I'd believe it from a stranger, it's so probable. Why shouldn't I believe it from you?'

(removes glasses, exits circle, still carrying book,
and walks anti-clockwise around the circumference)

ACTOR

My brother was killed in a hang-gliding accident in Australia in 1998 when he was 37. He was flying and he dropped. My father couldn't bear to come to Australia for the funeral so I came out with my family, my mother and my brother and we met my sister and her partner and my nephew who live in Katoomba, and we cremated him and scattered his ashes in the sky and went home to where my father was creating his unconventional relationship with the characters in the TV series. Shortly afterwards, he had a stroke and he began his long fall, which landed just before Christmas on the day I said I wouldn't come to Australia to do this art piece, which I didn't know what it was, which started with me telling you about telling my daughter about why I created this storm and why we're on this island...

(steps back inside the circle, spiralling once round its circumference to reach the microphone in the centre)

ACTOR

'Now, my excellent friend,' said my companion, 'You are in possession of all you need to follow my argument. We see that in the organic world, as reflection grows dimmer and weaker, grace emerges more brilliantly and decisively. But that is not all; two lines intersect, separate and pass through infinity and beyond, only to suddenly reappear at the same point of intersection. Or as we look into a concave mirror, our image vanishes into infinity only to turn up again right in front of us. So grace itself returns when self-consciousness has, as it were, gone through infinity. Grace appears most purely in that human form which either has no consciousness or an infinite consciousness. That is, in the puppet or in the god.'

'Does that mean,' I said in some bewilderment, 'that we must eat again of the tree of knowledge in order to return to the state of innocence?'

'Of course,' he said, 'But that's the final chapter in the history of the world.'

(snaps book shut)

Camera A. Roll 5. End board.

(actor takes four bows)

(clapper)

Camera B. Roll 5. End board.

(as he exits the circle and the theatre)

Adapted transcript of the four filmed live performances of *Event for a Stage*, Carriageworks, Sydney, 2014. Co-commissioned by 19th Biennale of Sydney. Written in collaboration with Stephen Dillane.

Reading from *On the Marionette Theatre*, Heinrich von Kleist, 1810. Adapted from a translation by Idris Parry in *Hand to Mouth and Other Essays*, Carcanet Press, 1981.

Event for a Stage, 2015
16mm colour film, optical sound,
50 minutes

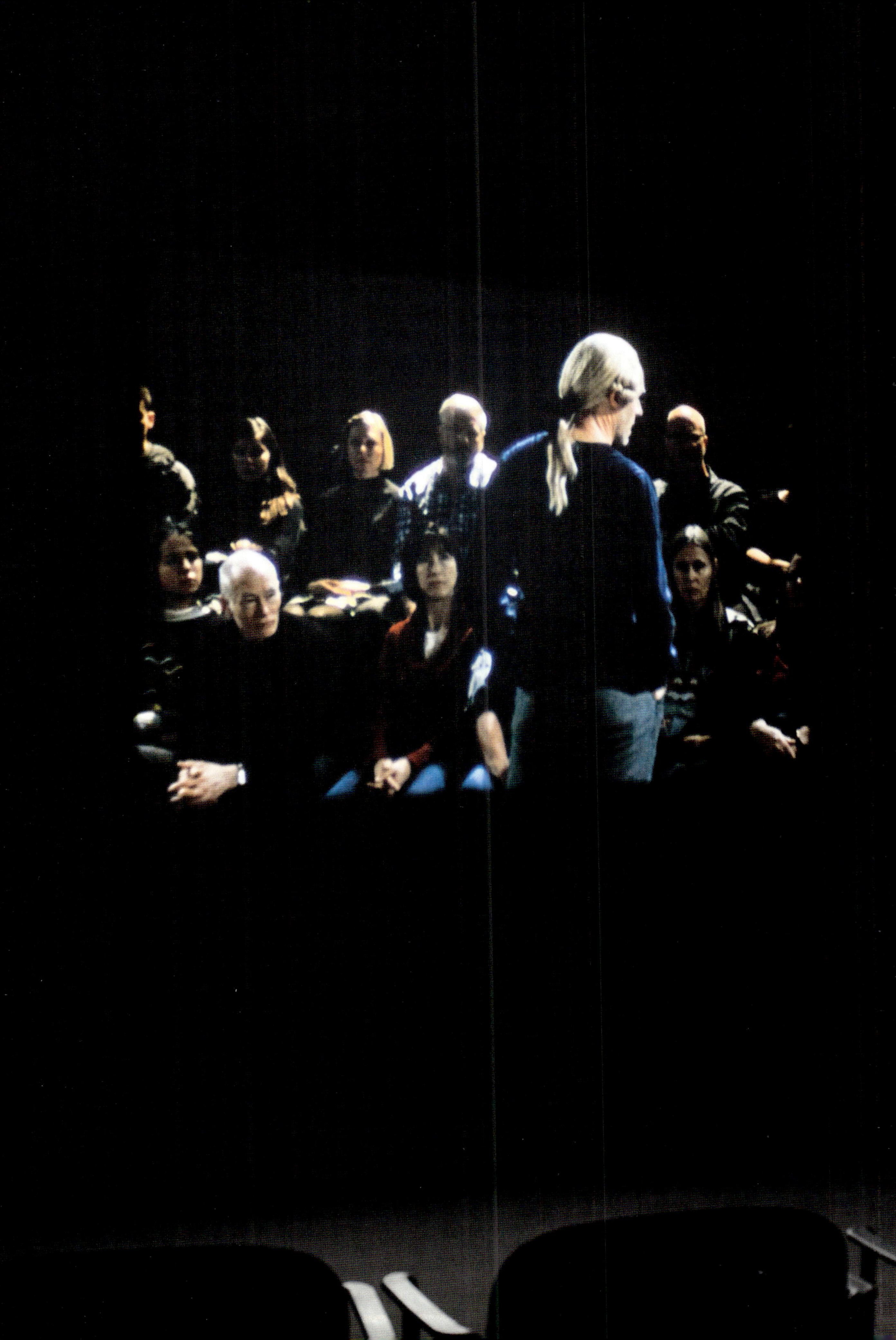

Event for a Stage, 2014
Gouache on found postcard, used for the poster for *Event for a Stage*, Carriageworks, May 2014
8.6 x 13.7 cm

overleaf:
When first I raised the Tempest, 2016
Chalk on blackboard
244 x 976 cm

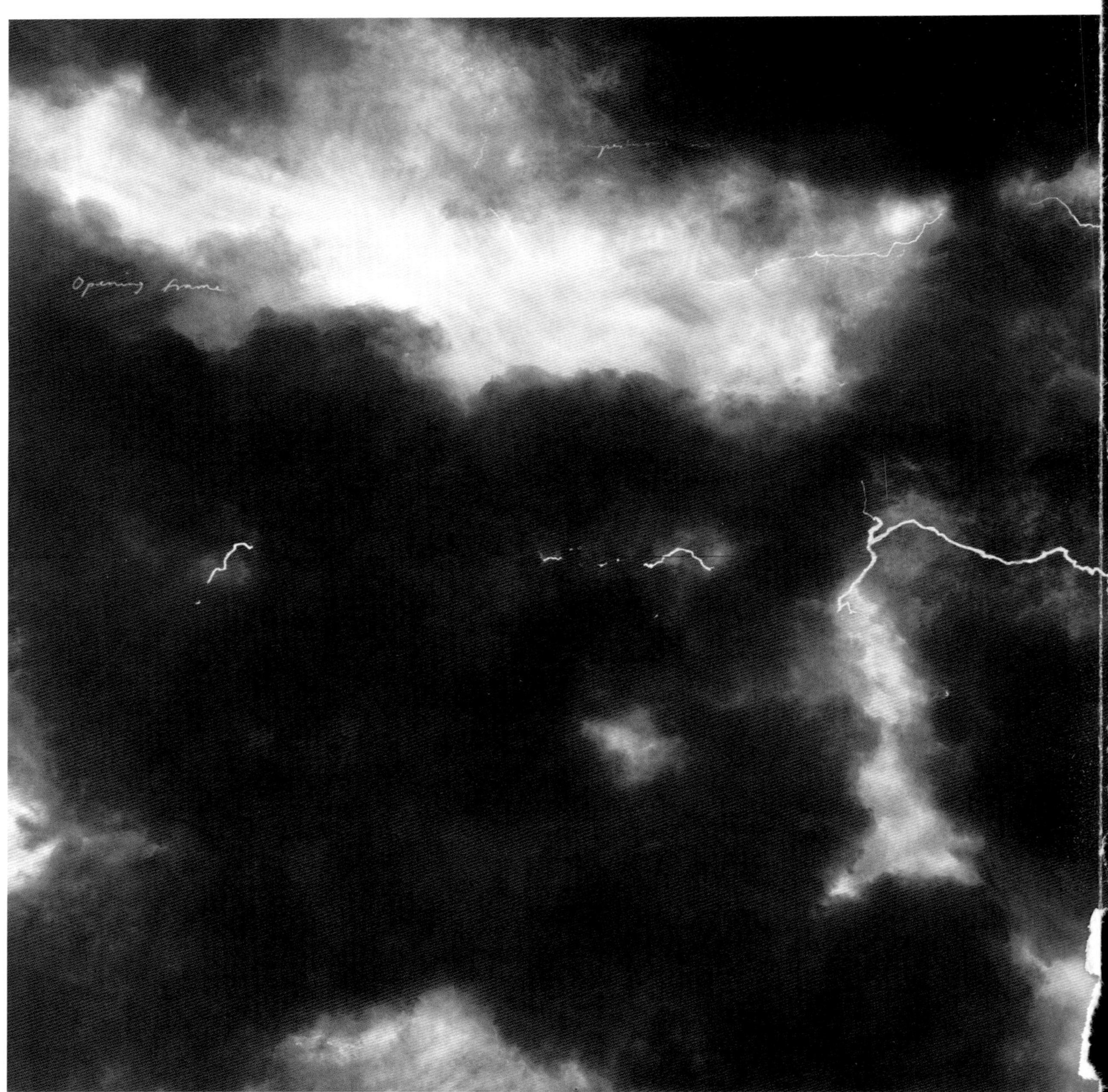
Opening frame

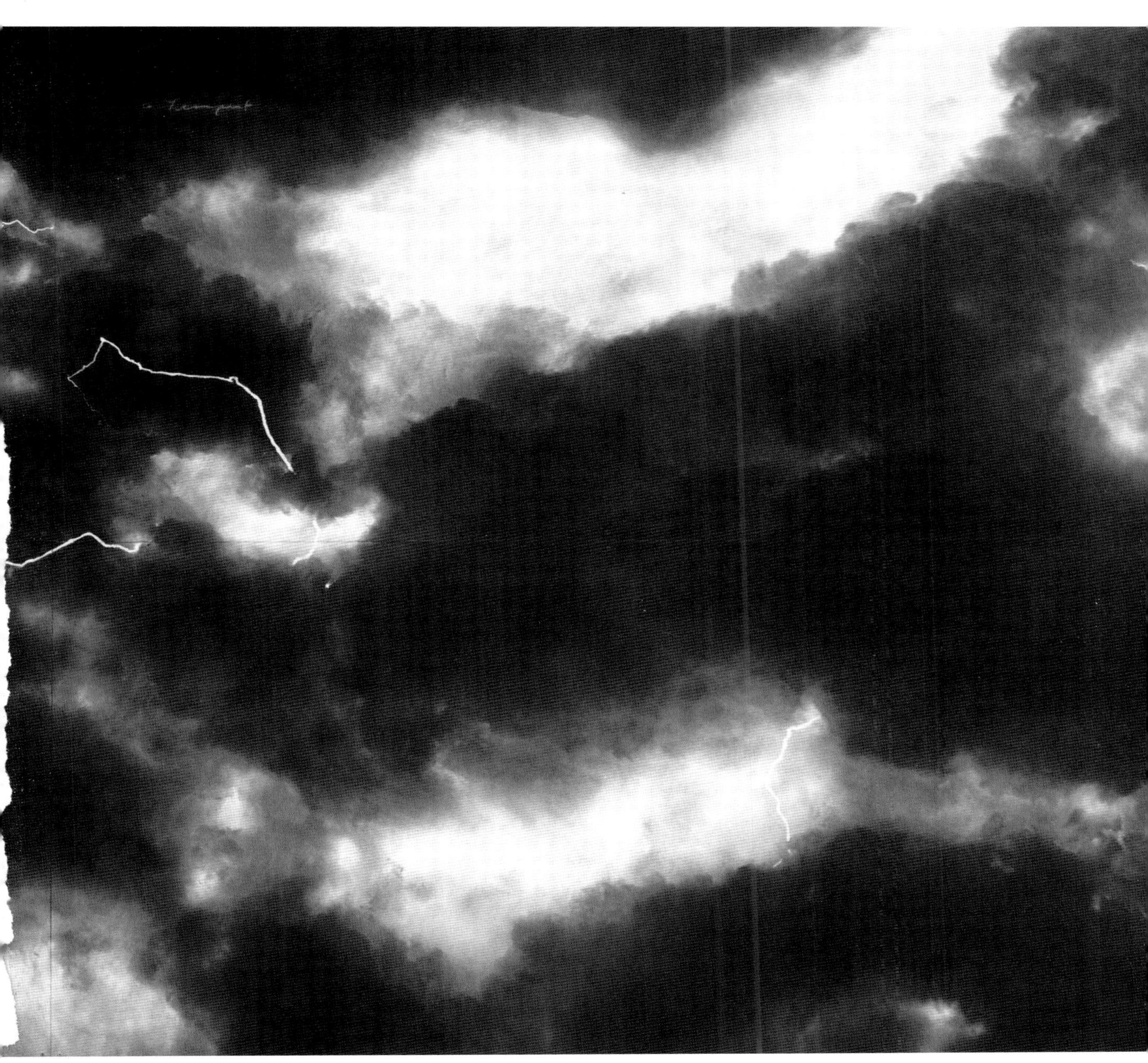

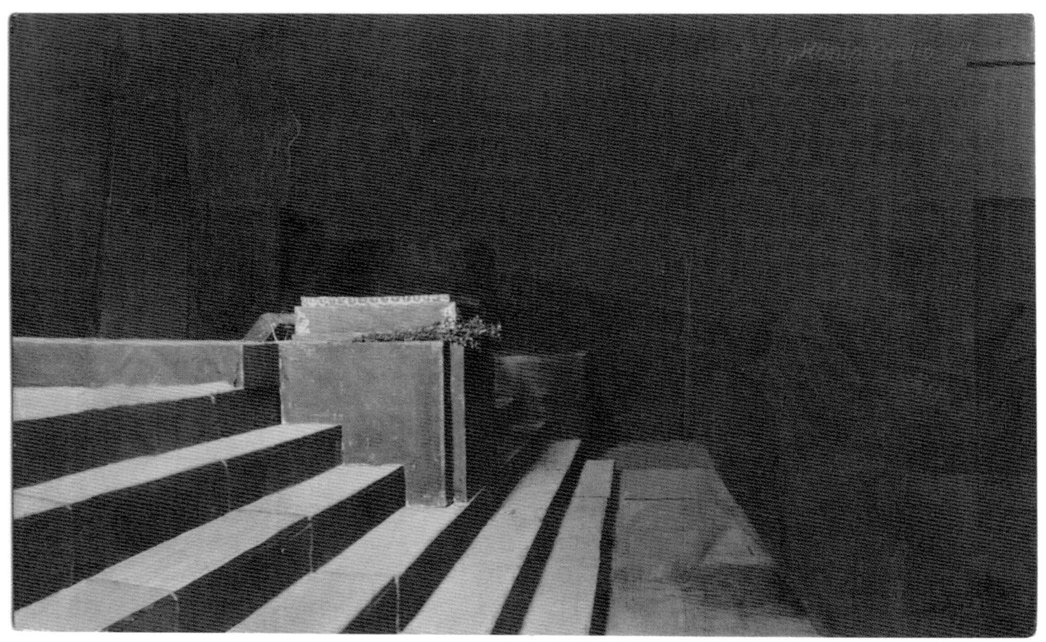

His Picture in Little, 2017 (film stills)
35mm colour anamorphic film,
silent, reduced to spherical 16mm
for exhibition as a miniature,
15½ minutes, continuous loop

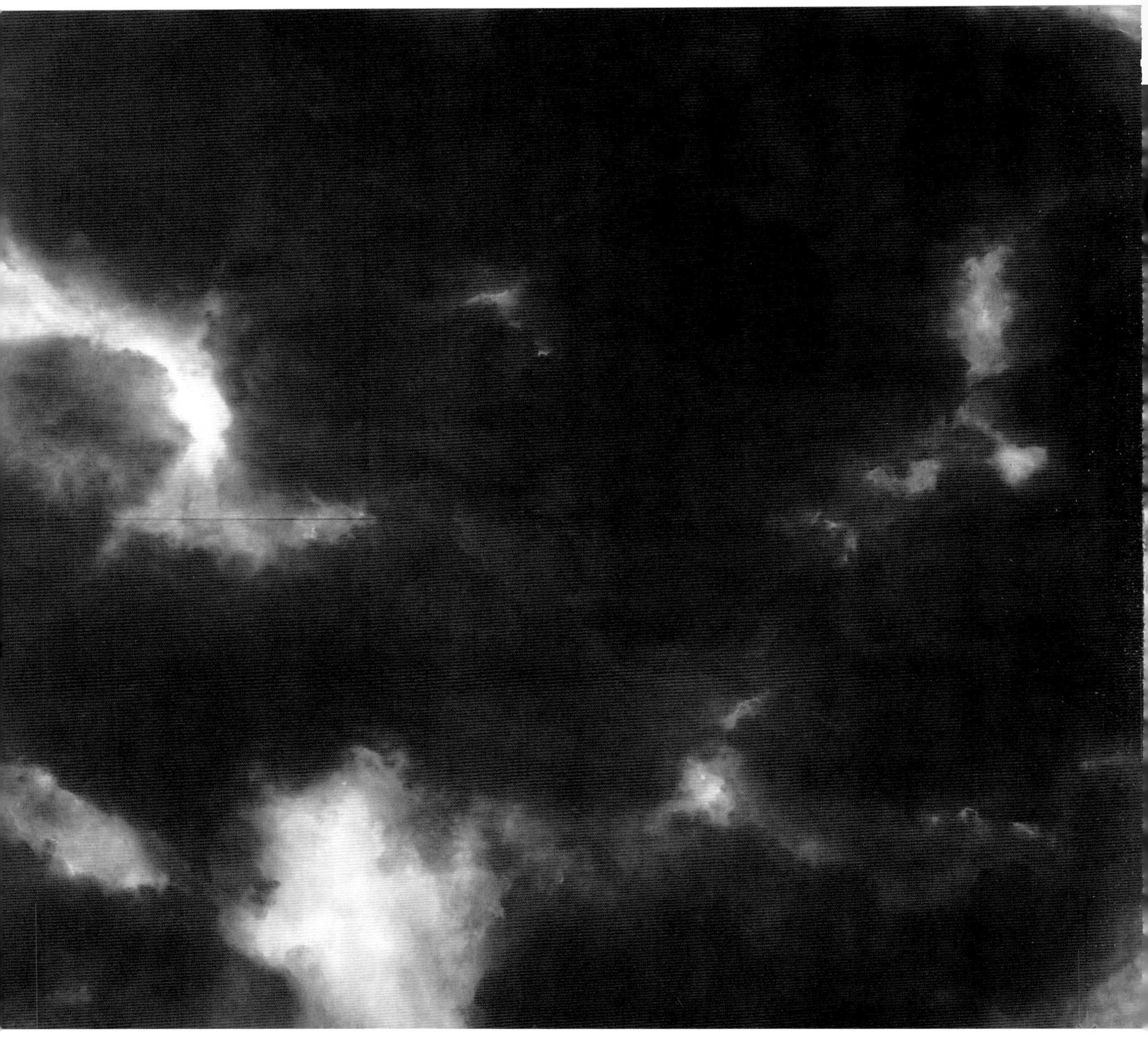

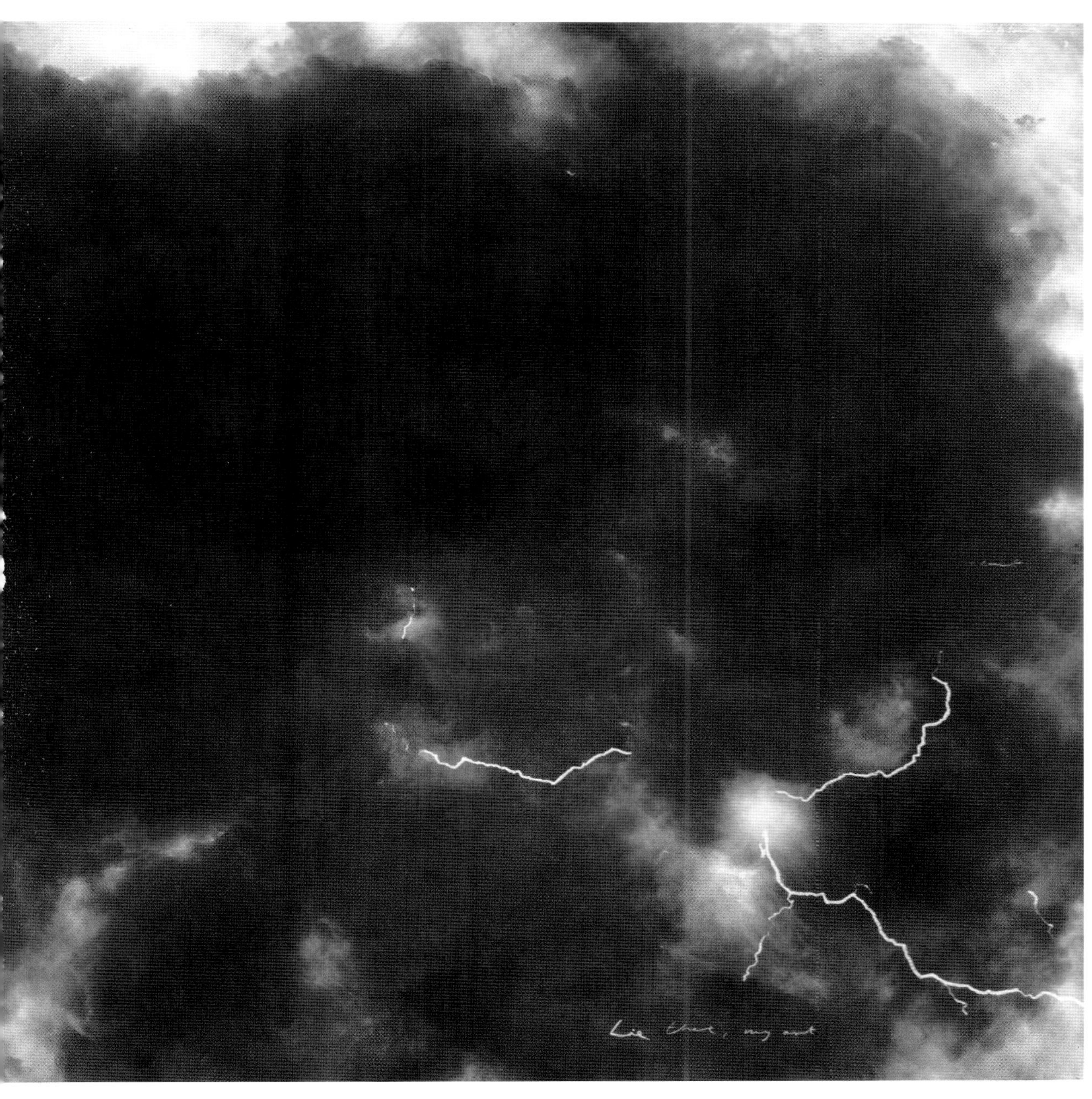
Lie there, my art

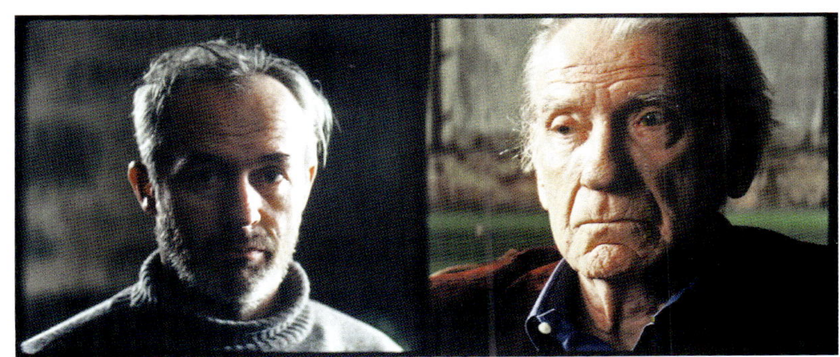
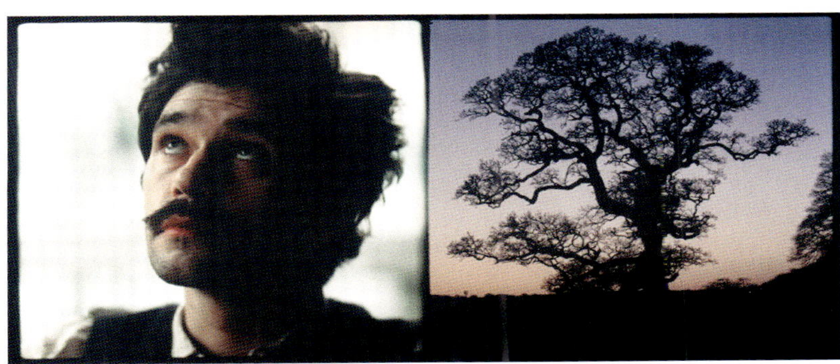
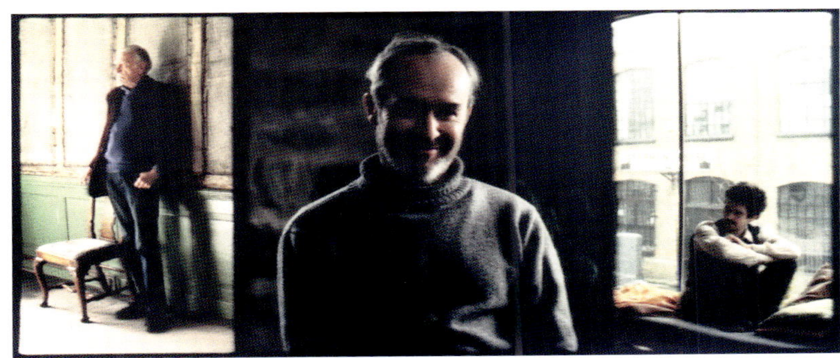
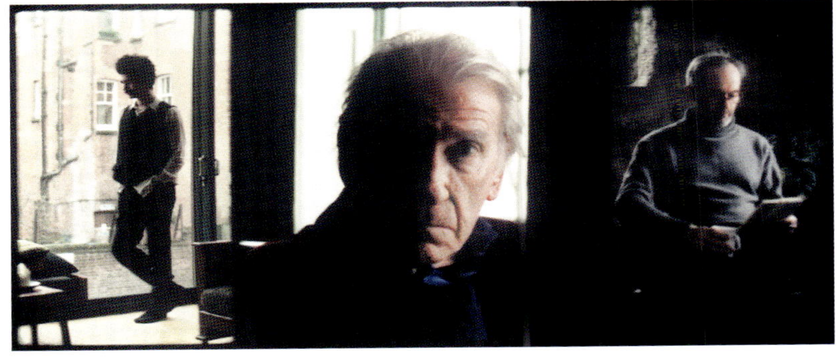
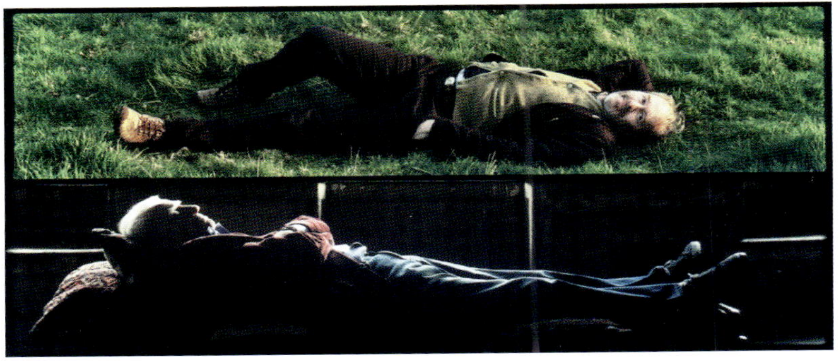

Providence, 2017 (film stills)
35mm colour anamorphic film, silent,
reduced to spherical 16mm for exhibition,
5½ minutes, continuous loop

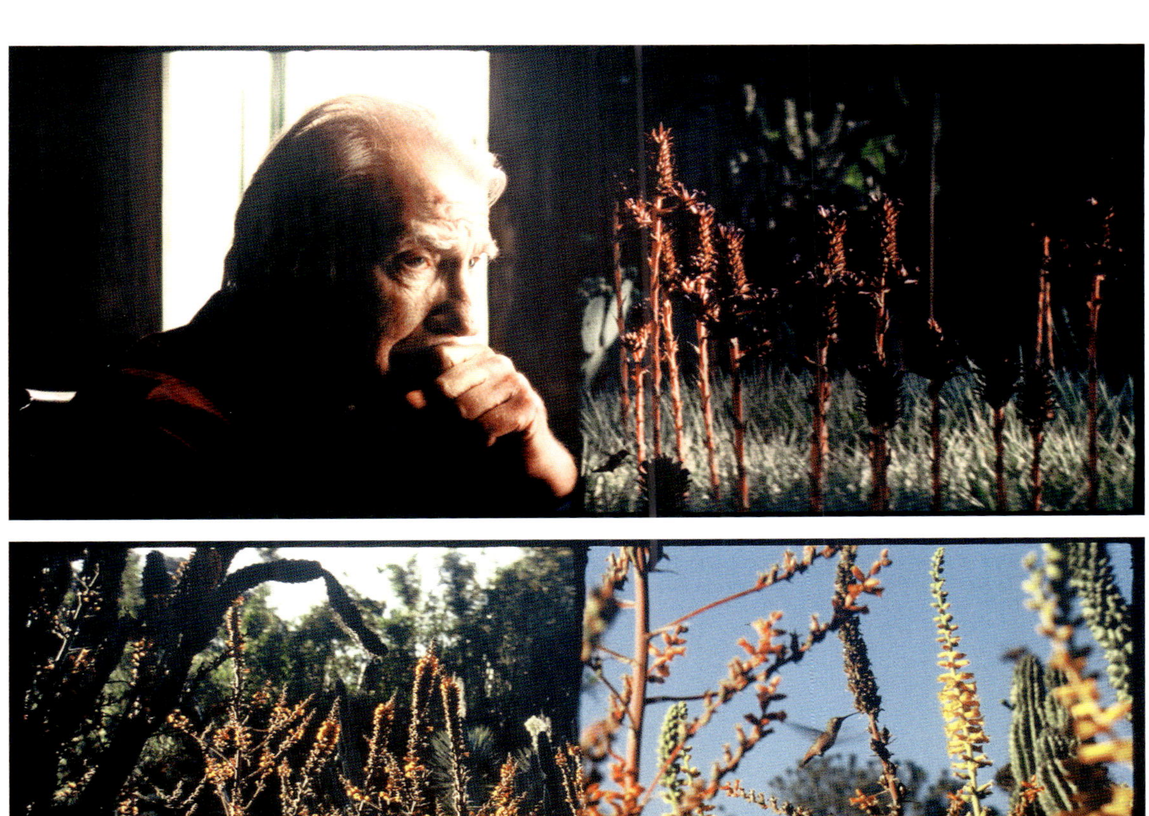

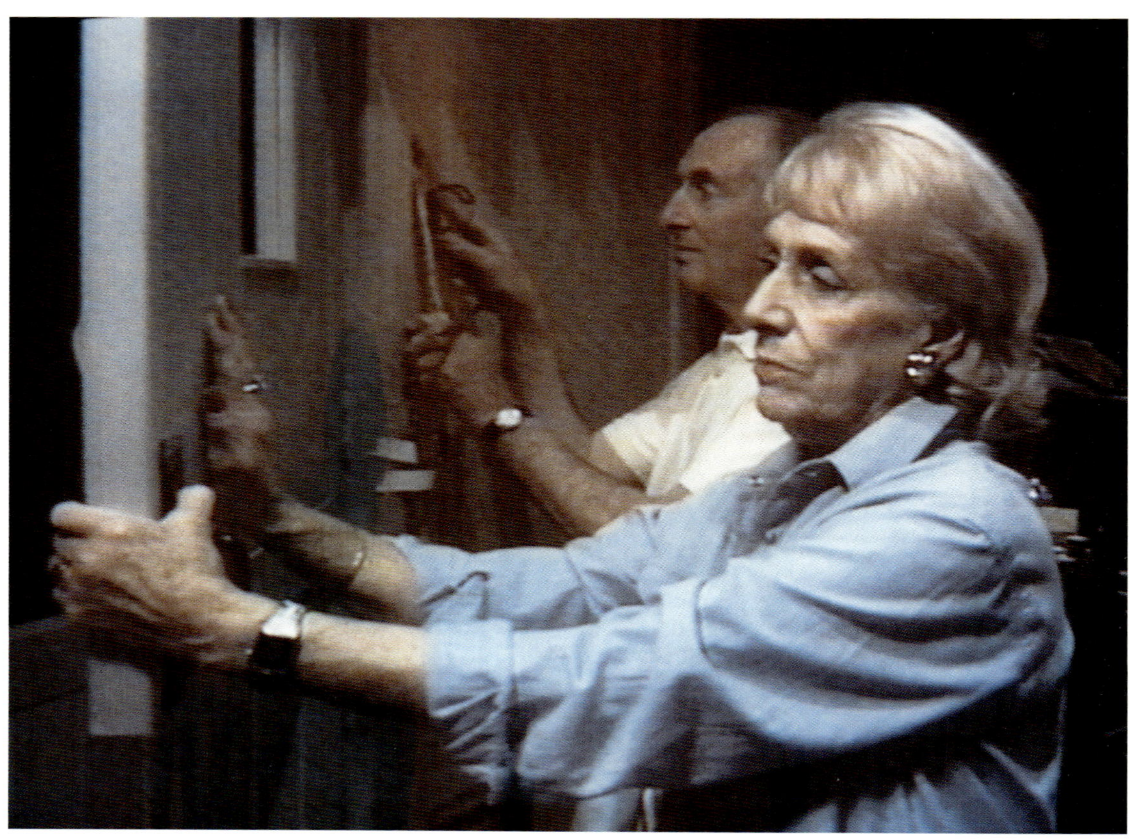

ROOM LOCKER UMBRE

FOOTSTEPS ON BOARDS CROSS FADE → 2

OPEN DOOR + F/STEPS ON CARPET

F/STEPS ON CARPET

OPEN DOOR + F/STEPS ON CARPET

OPEN DOOR

FOOTSTEPS ON STAIRS

F/STEPS ON TILE

LO

FOOTSTEPS ON BOARDS CROSS FADE ← 1

SWING DOOR

SWING DOOR

SWING DOOR

CIST

VOICE "OPEN YOUR EARS..."

VOICE "I, FROM THE ORIENT..." C/FADE → 7

CISTE

VEL

VOICE "OPEN MY TONGUES..." C/FADE ← 6

RAI

NOISE ← 7

VOICE "...BALL OF EARTH..."

F/STEPS ON STAIRS REVERB

RAI

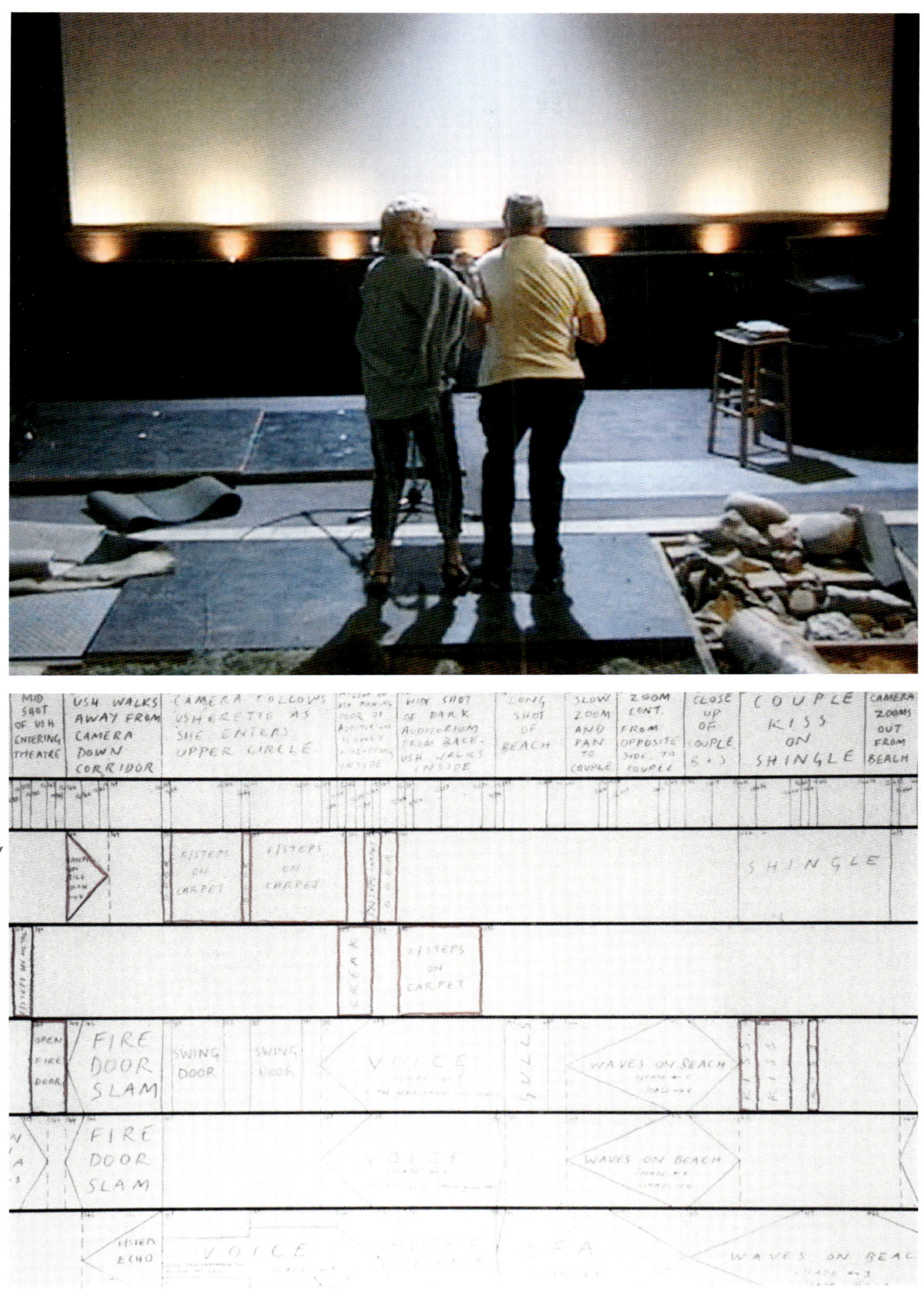

Foley Artist, 1996 (video stills and details of dubbing chart)
Laserdisc and monitor, 8 speakers, Akai DD8 playback machine, Sondor magnetic playback machine, dubbing chart lightbox

The Russian Ending, 2001
Portfolio of 20 photogravures on
Hahnemühle Bütten 300g paper
Each 54 x 79.4 cm

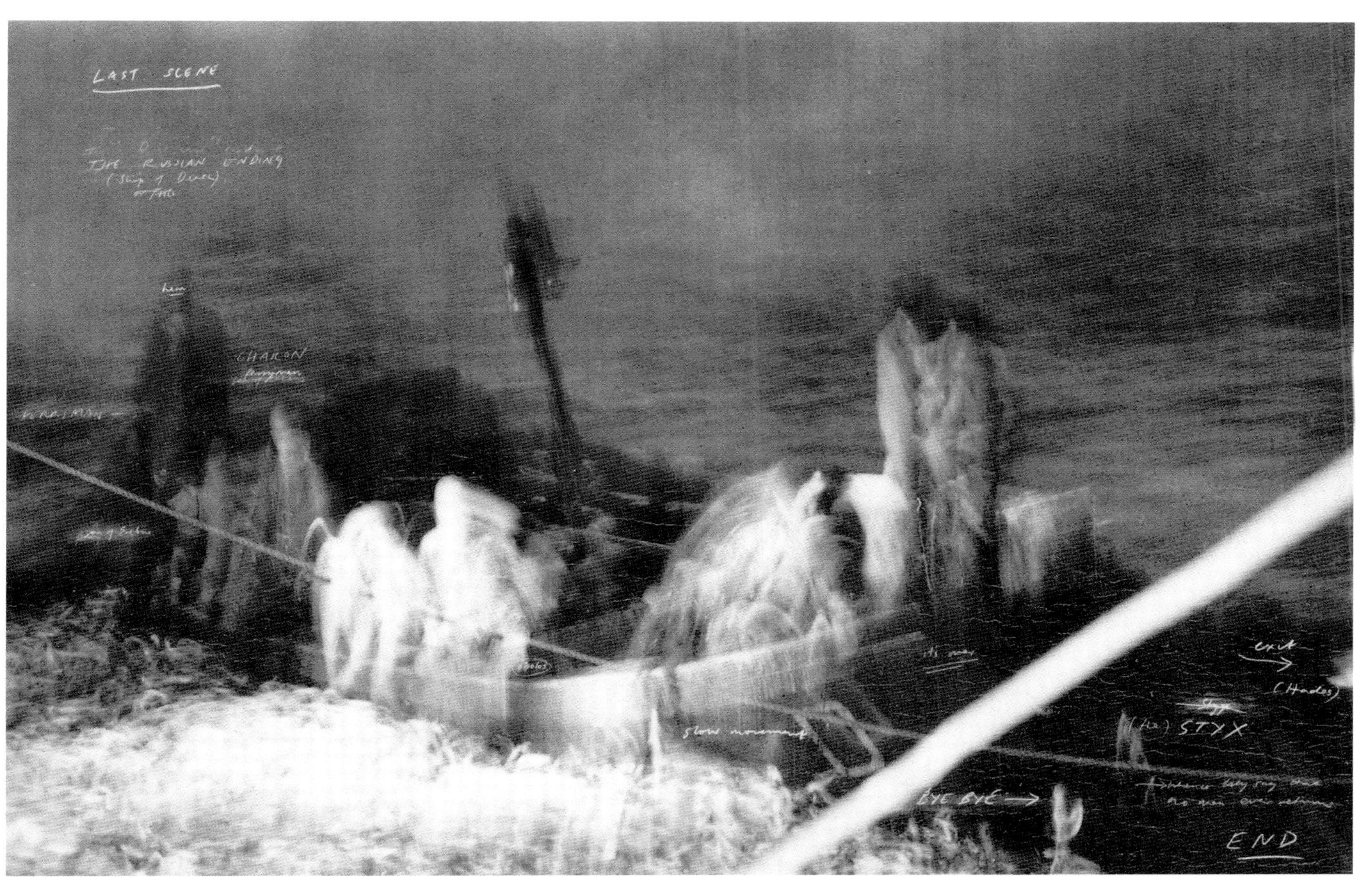
LAST SCENE
THE RUSSIAN ENDING
CHARON
slow movement
exit
(Hades)
STYX
BYE BYE
END

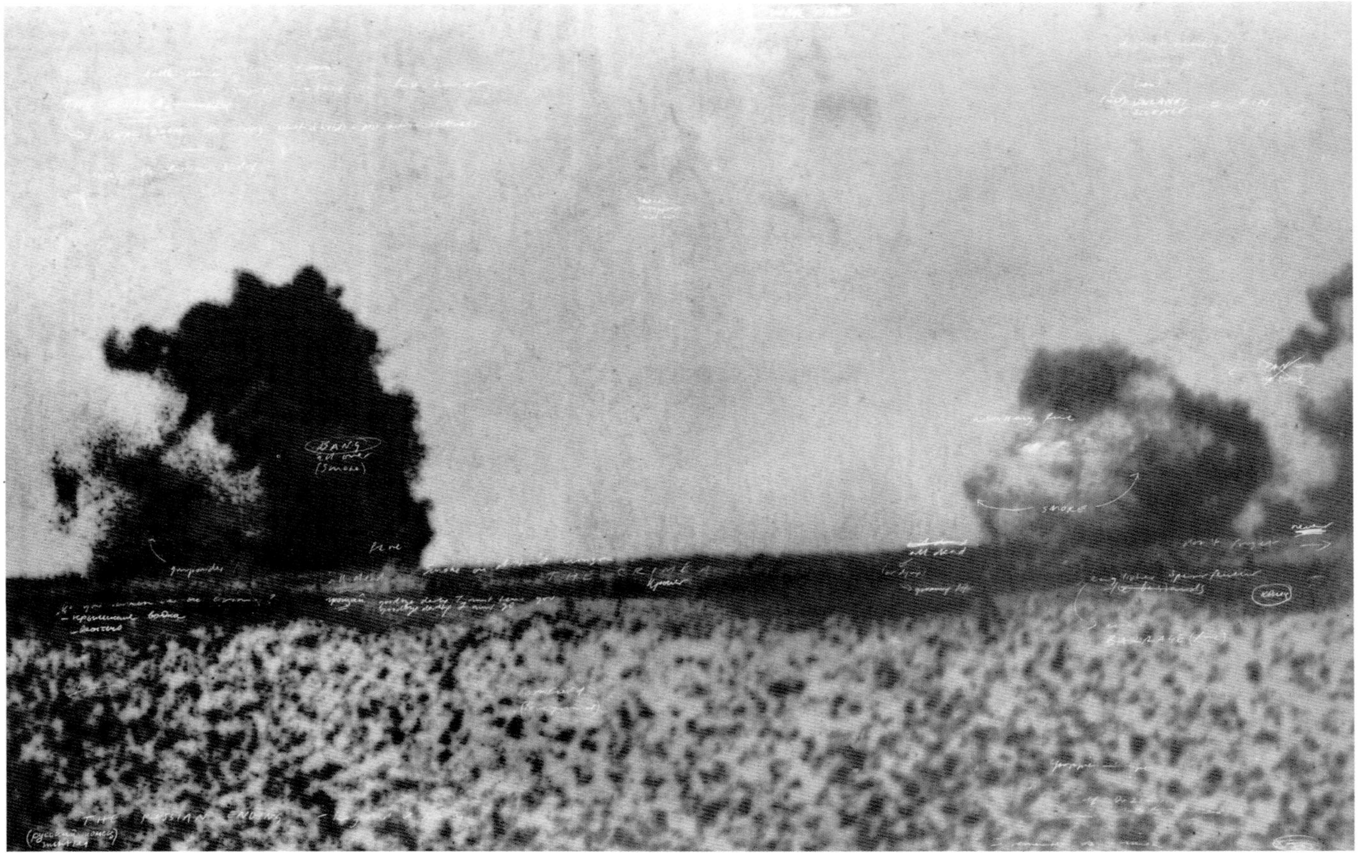

BANG

BARRAGE

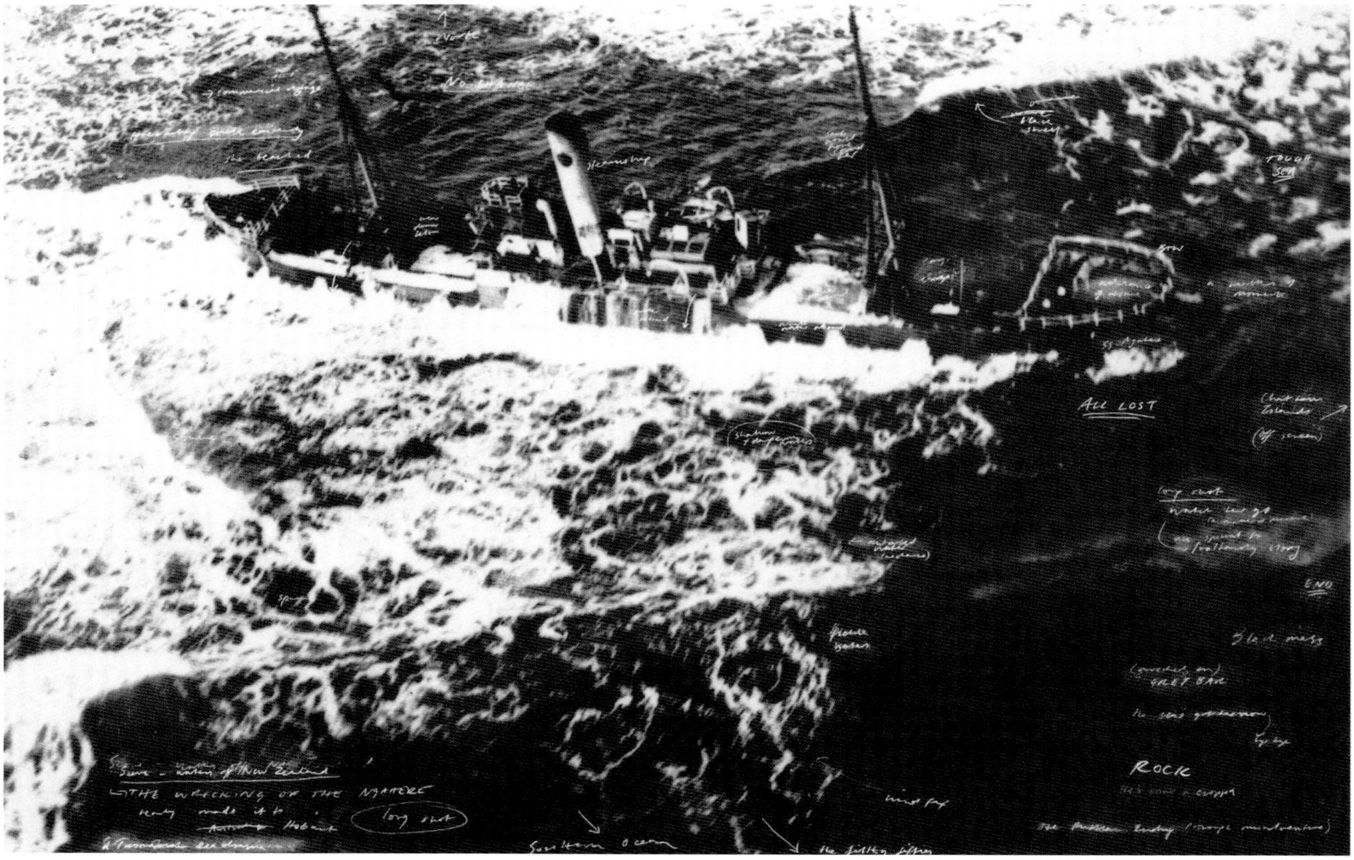

ALL LOST

(off screen)

long shot

END

GREY BAR

ROCK

long shot

Hobart

Southern Ocean

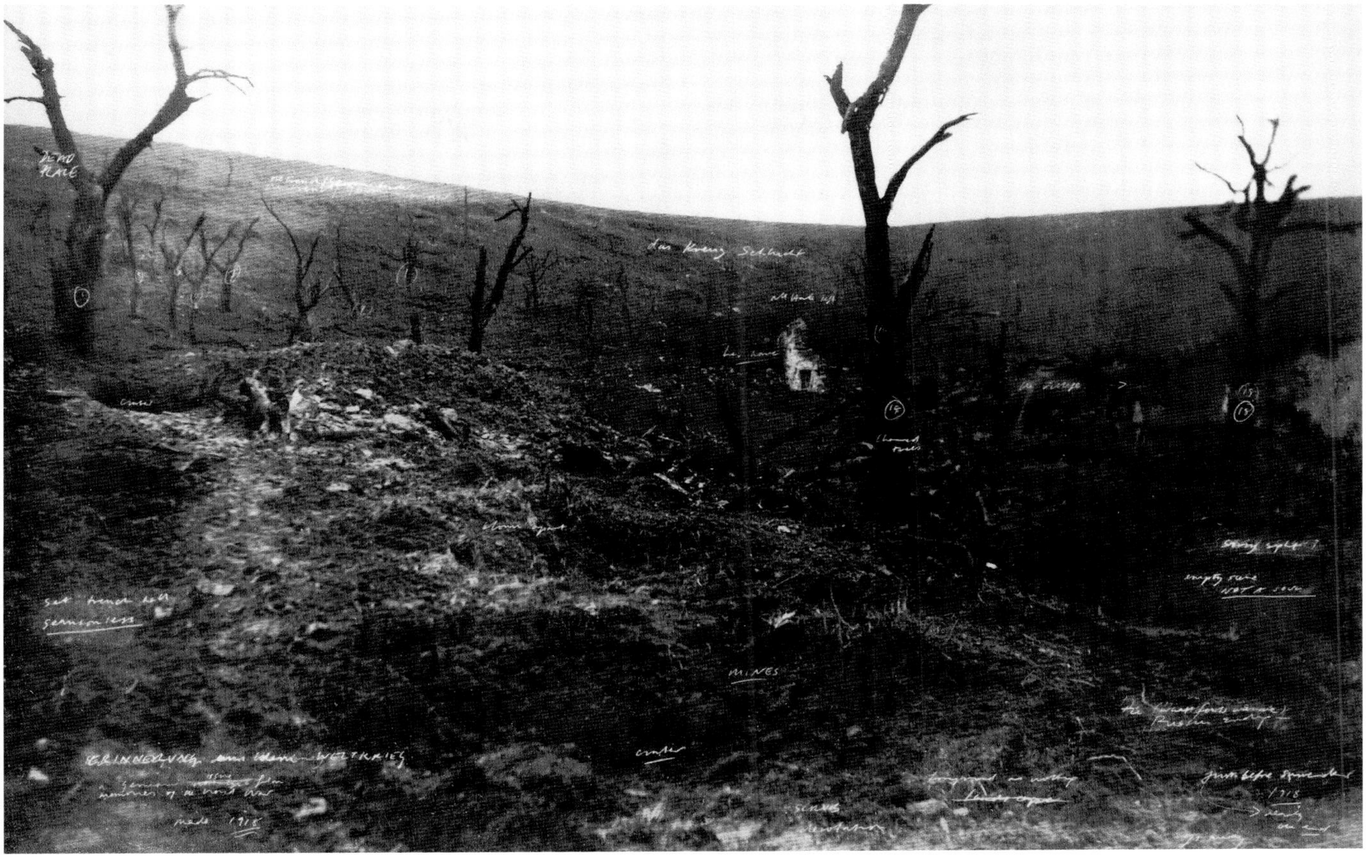

DEAD PLACE

MINES

crater

ERINNERUNG an den WELTKRIEG

memories of the World War

made 1918

just before surrender

1918

WESTERN FRONT

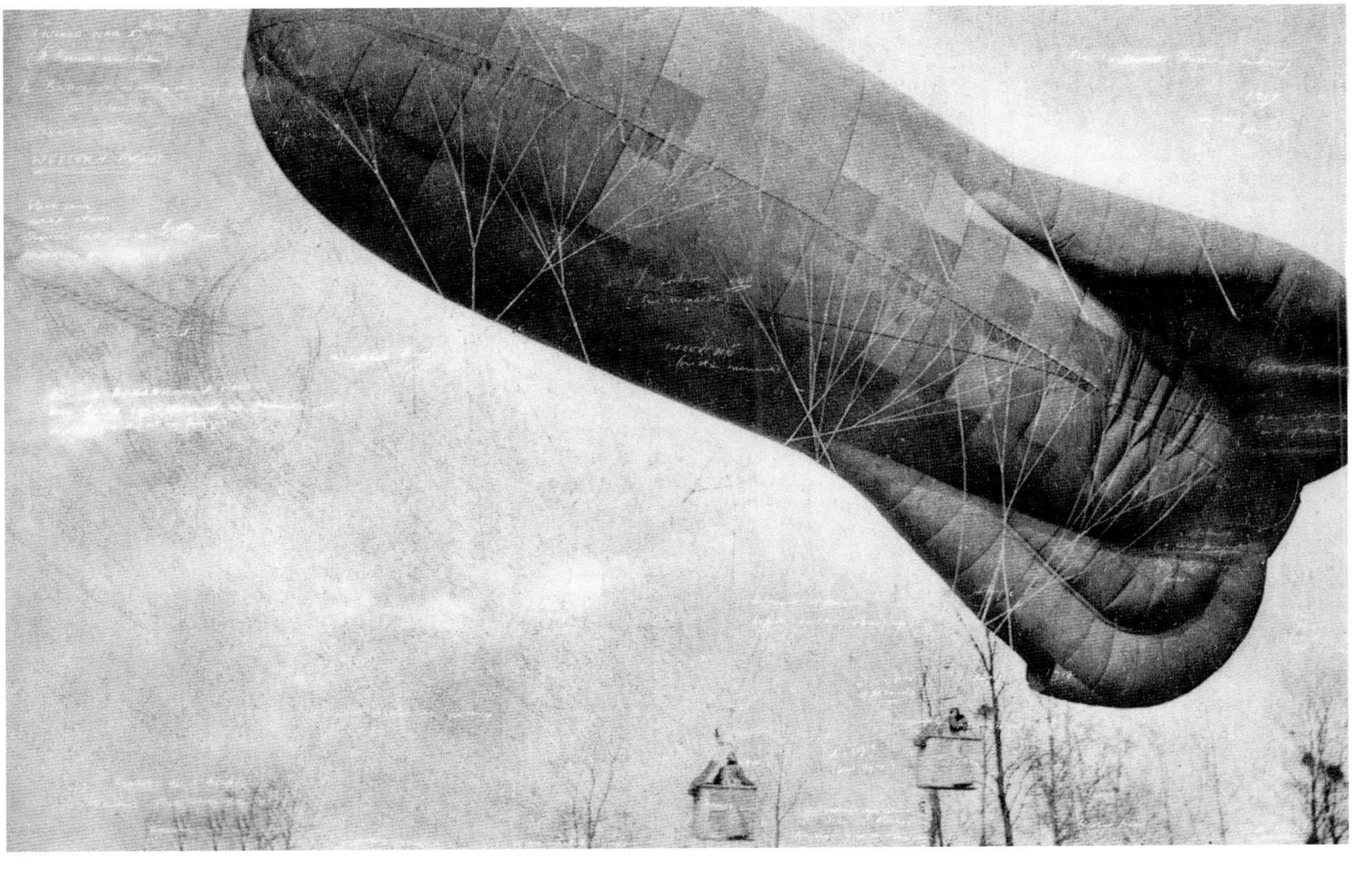

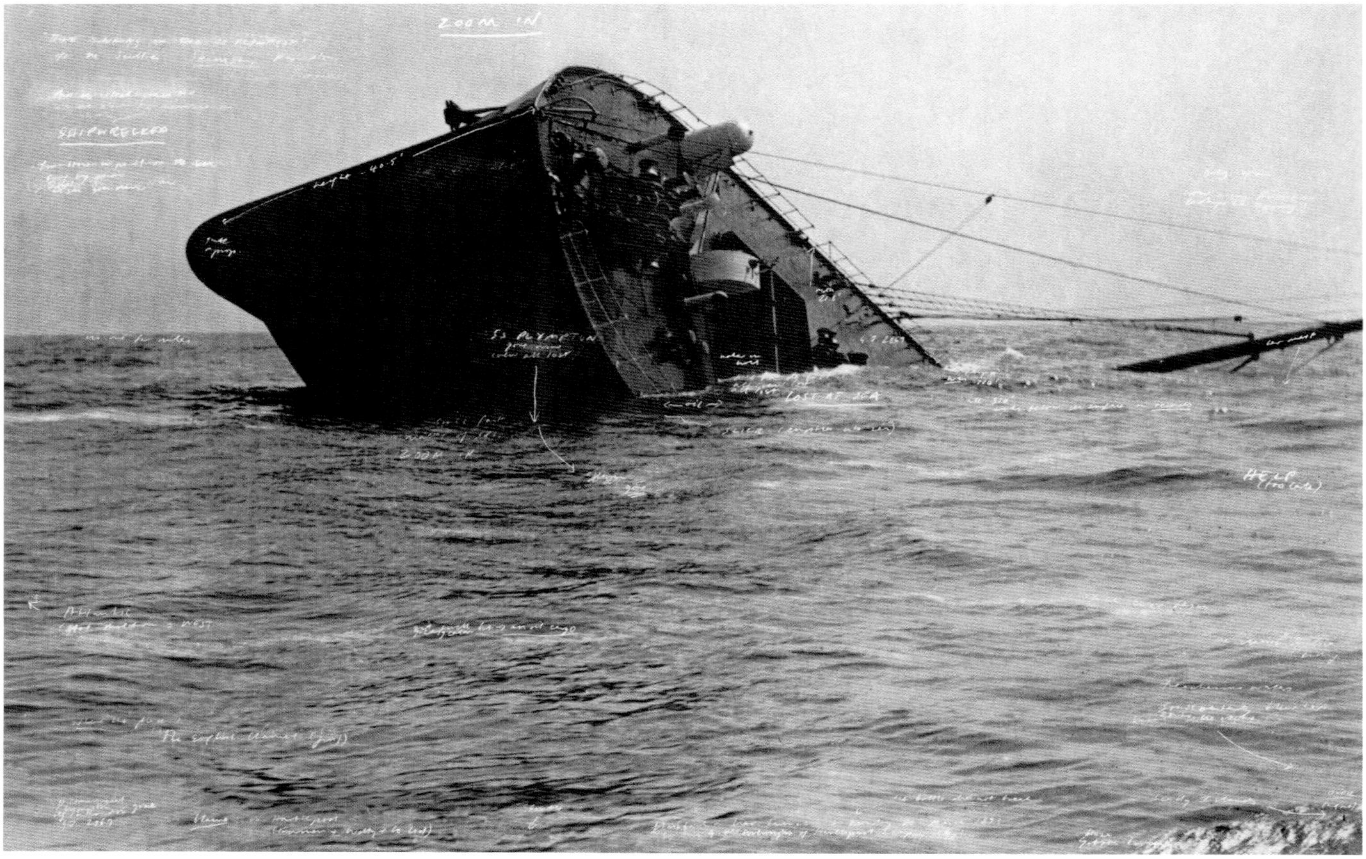

ZOOM IN

SHIPWRECKED

LOST AT SEA

HELP

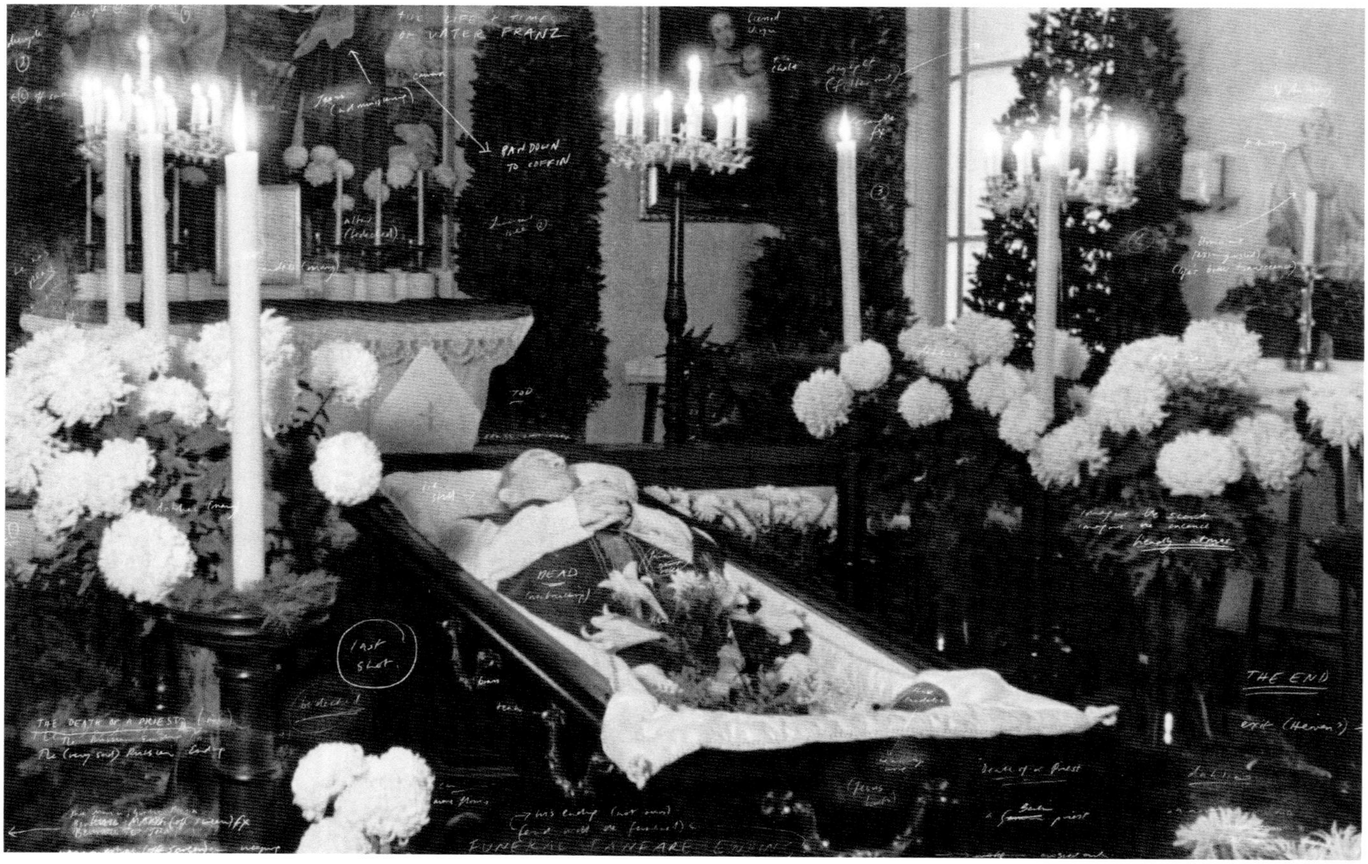

THE LIFE & TIMES OF VATER FRANZ

PAN DOWN TO COFFIN

DEAD

last shot

THE END

THE DEATH OF A PRIEST

Death of a Priest

FUNERAL FANFARE ENDING

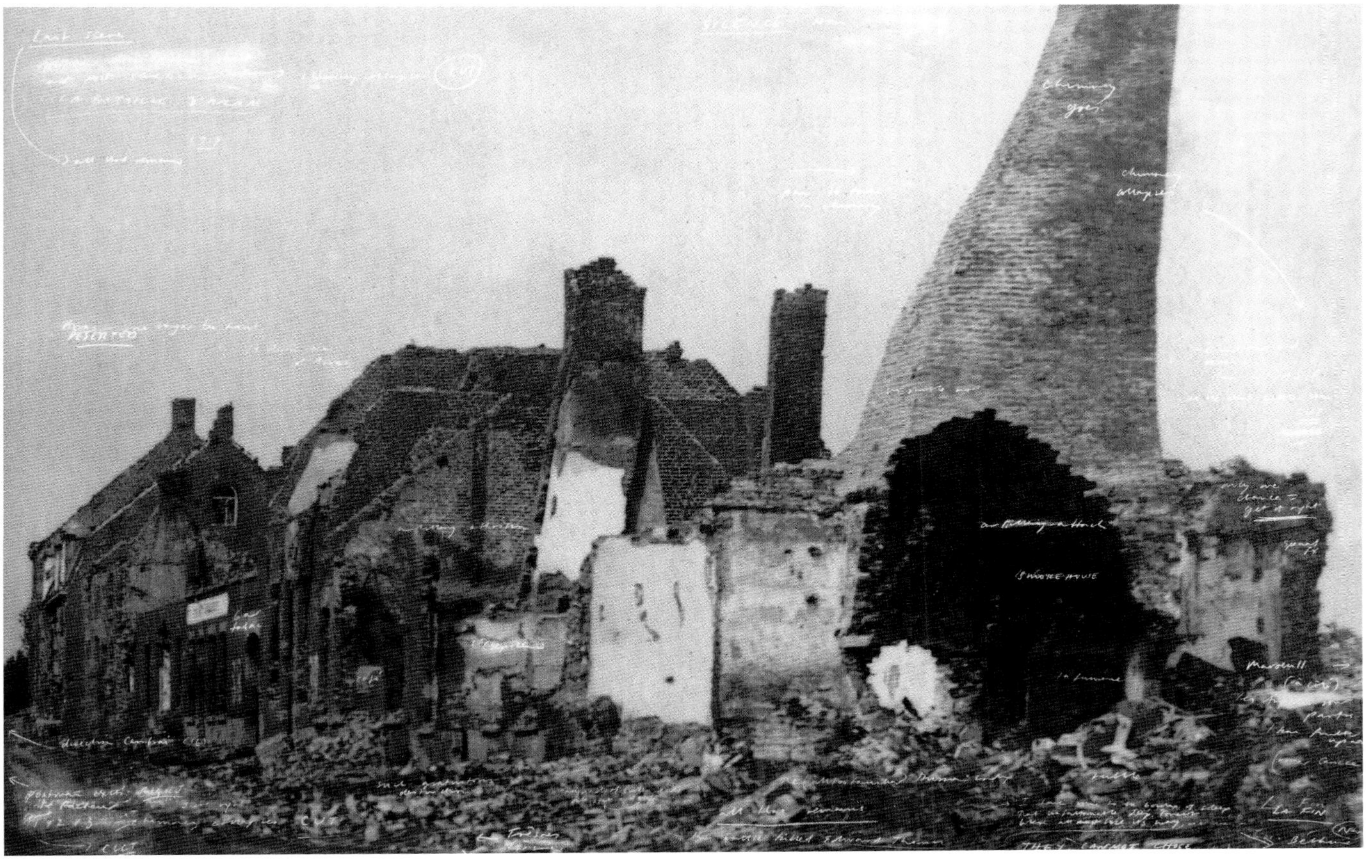
SMOKEHOUSE

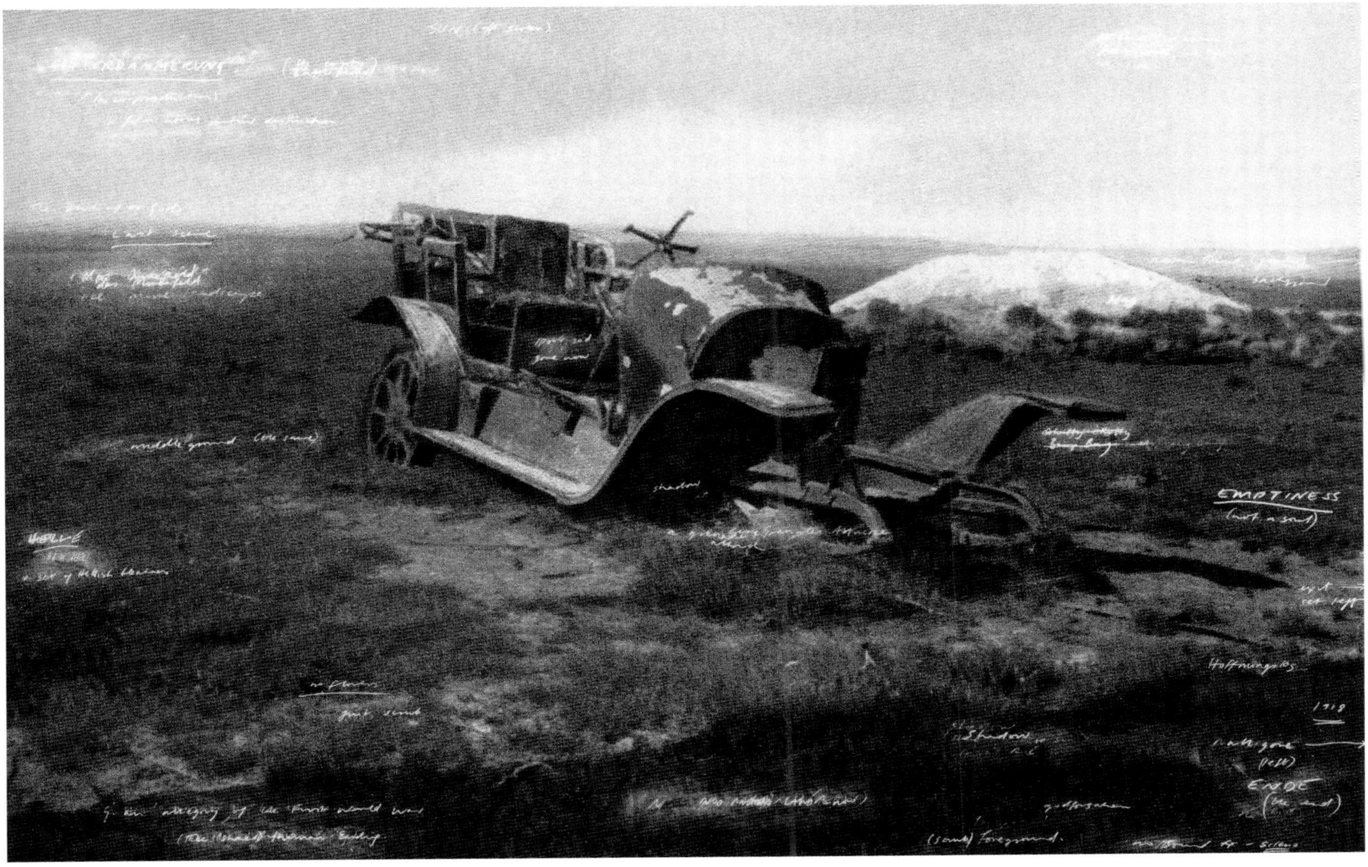
EMPTINESS
1918

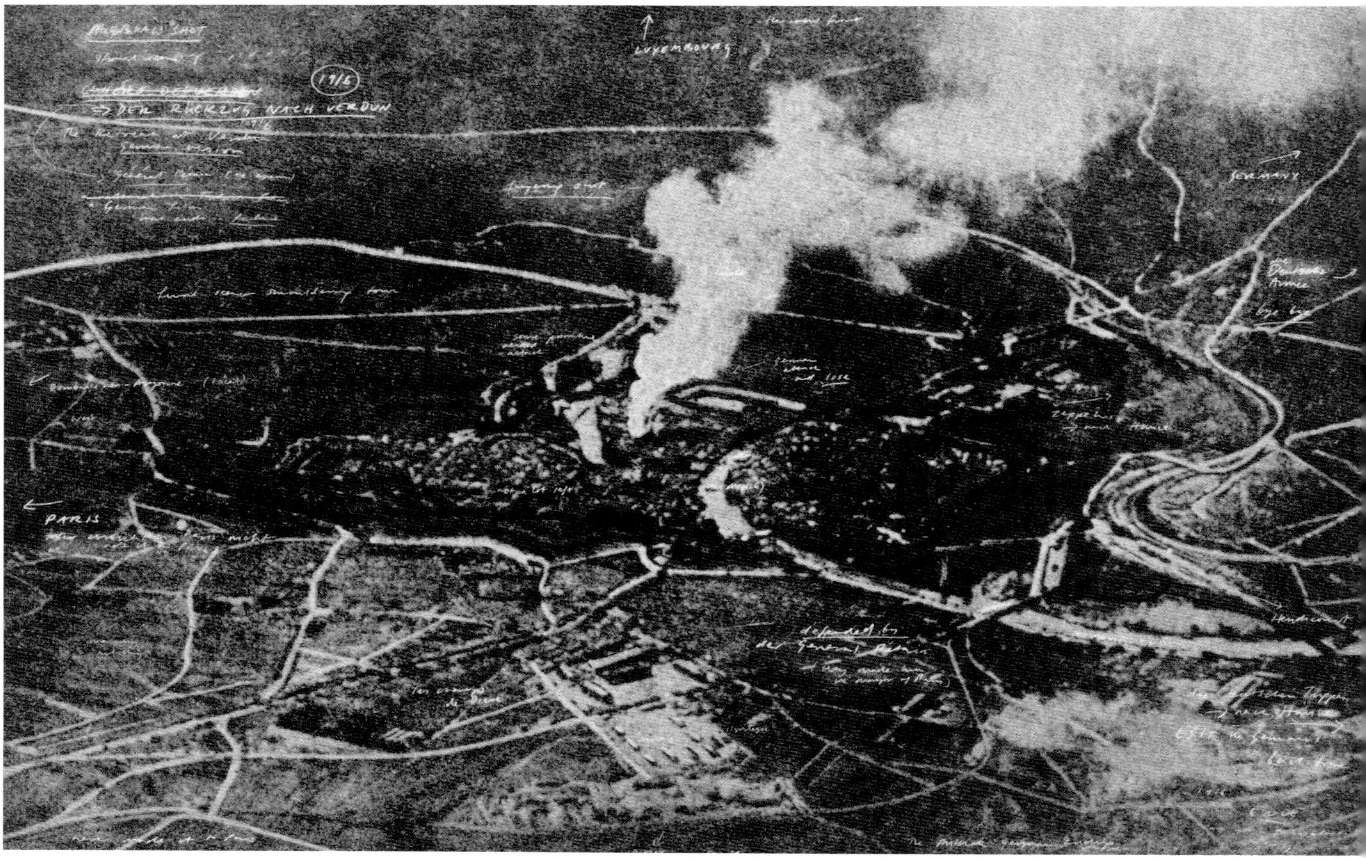

LUXEMBOURG

1916

DER RHEINZUG NACH VERDUN

GERMANY

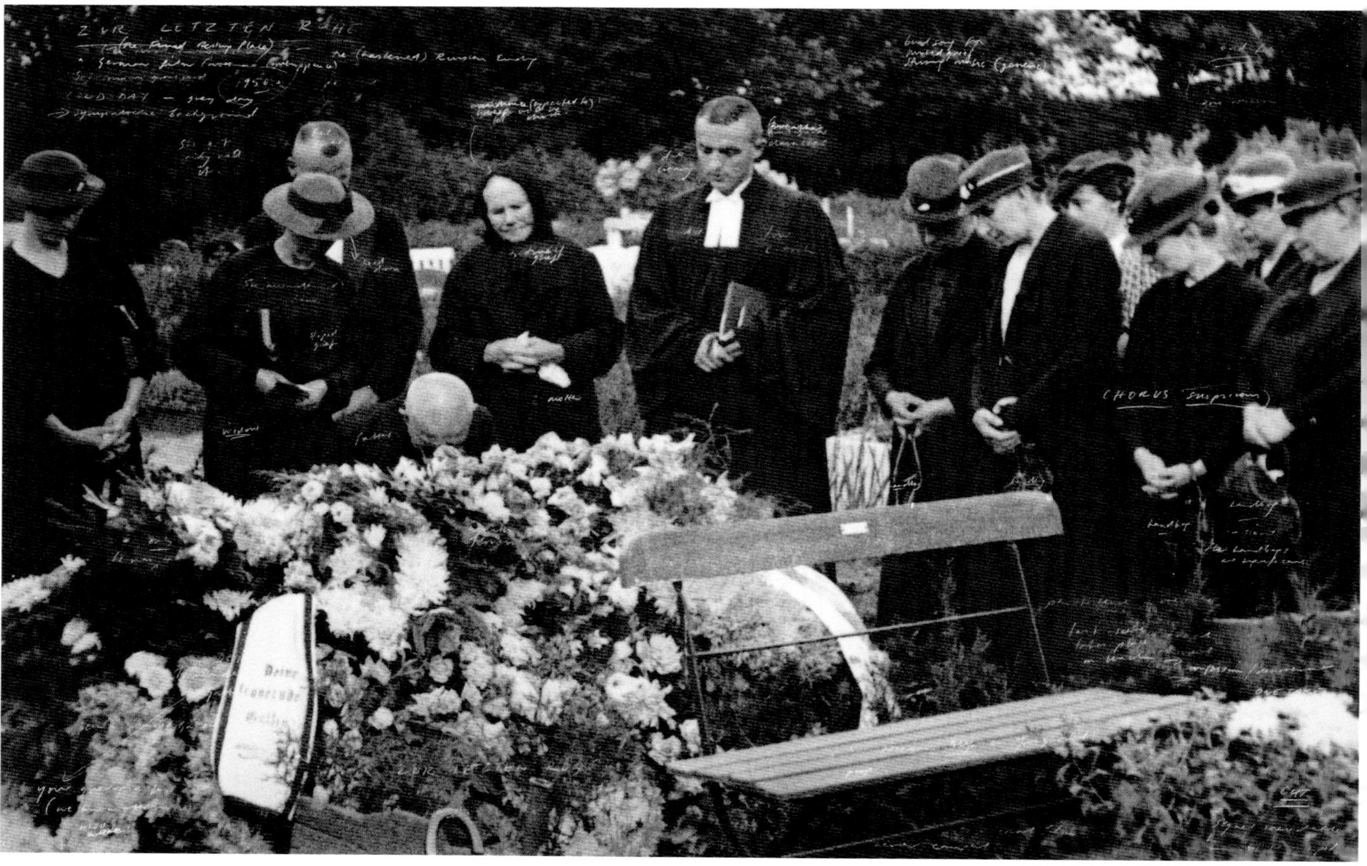

PARIS

ZUR LETZTEN RUHE

1950

CHORUS

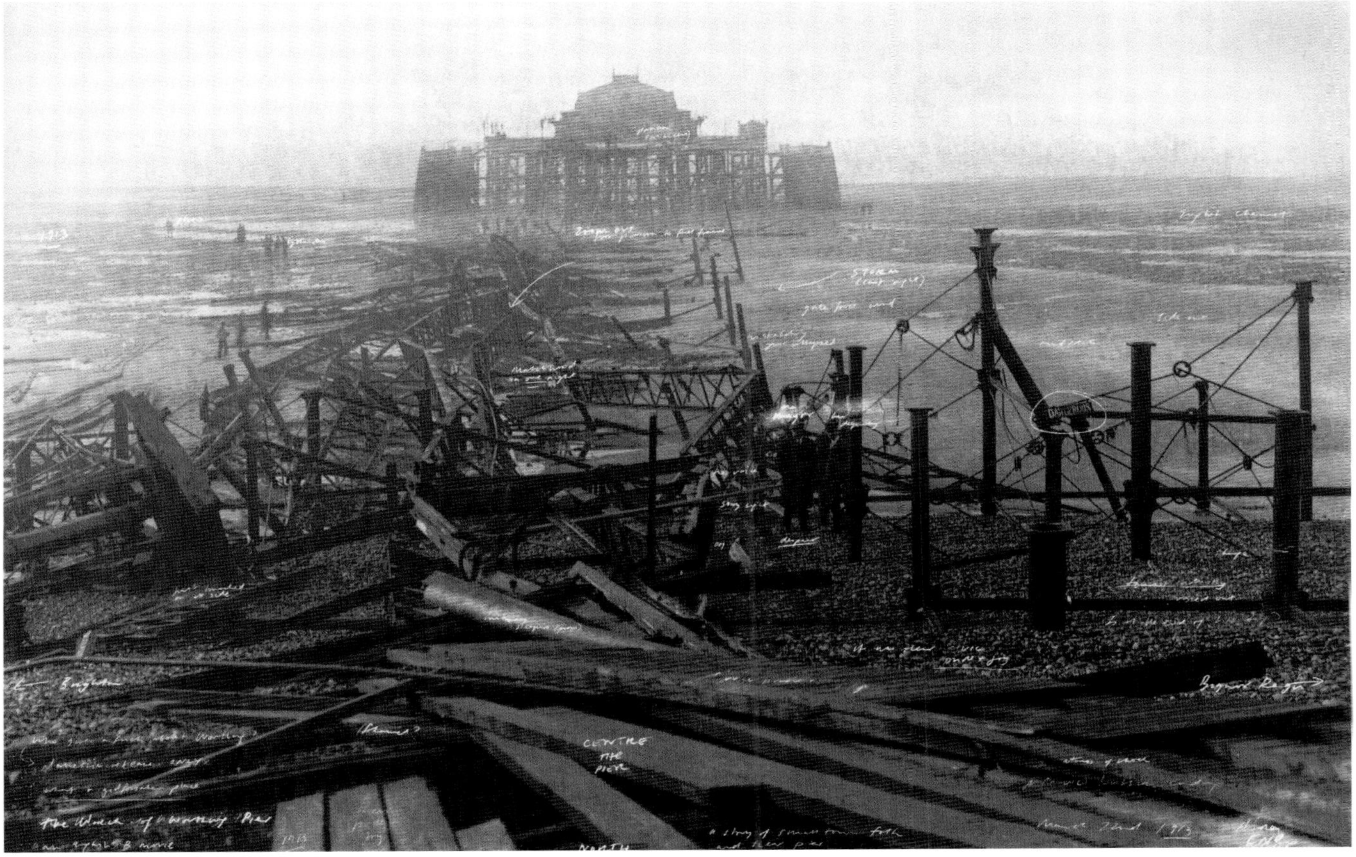

CENTRE
THE
PIER

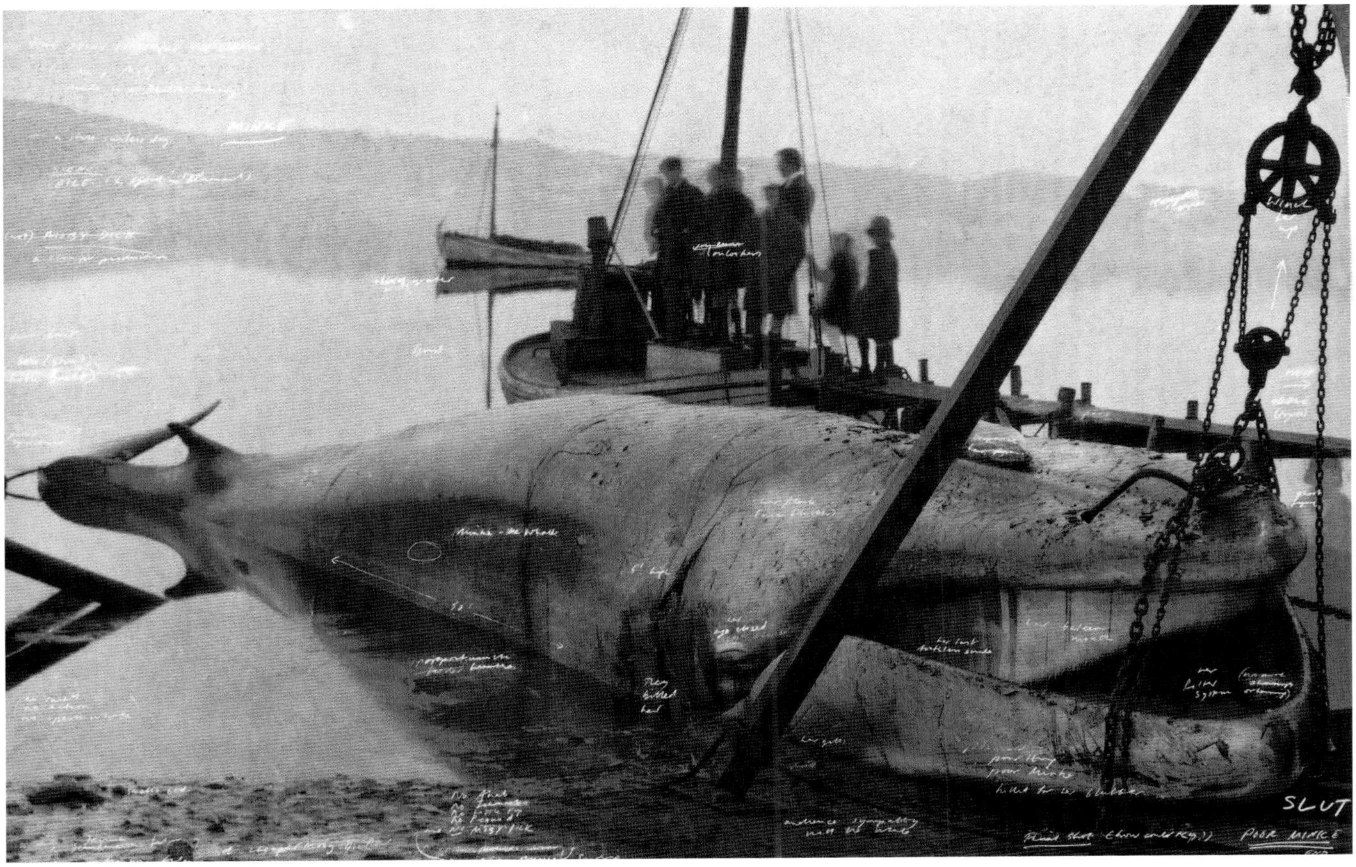

SLUT

POOR MINKE

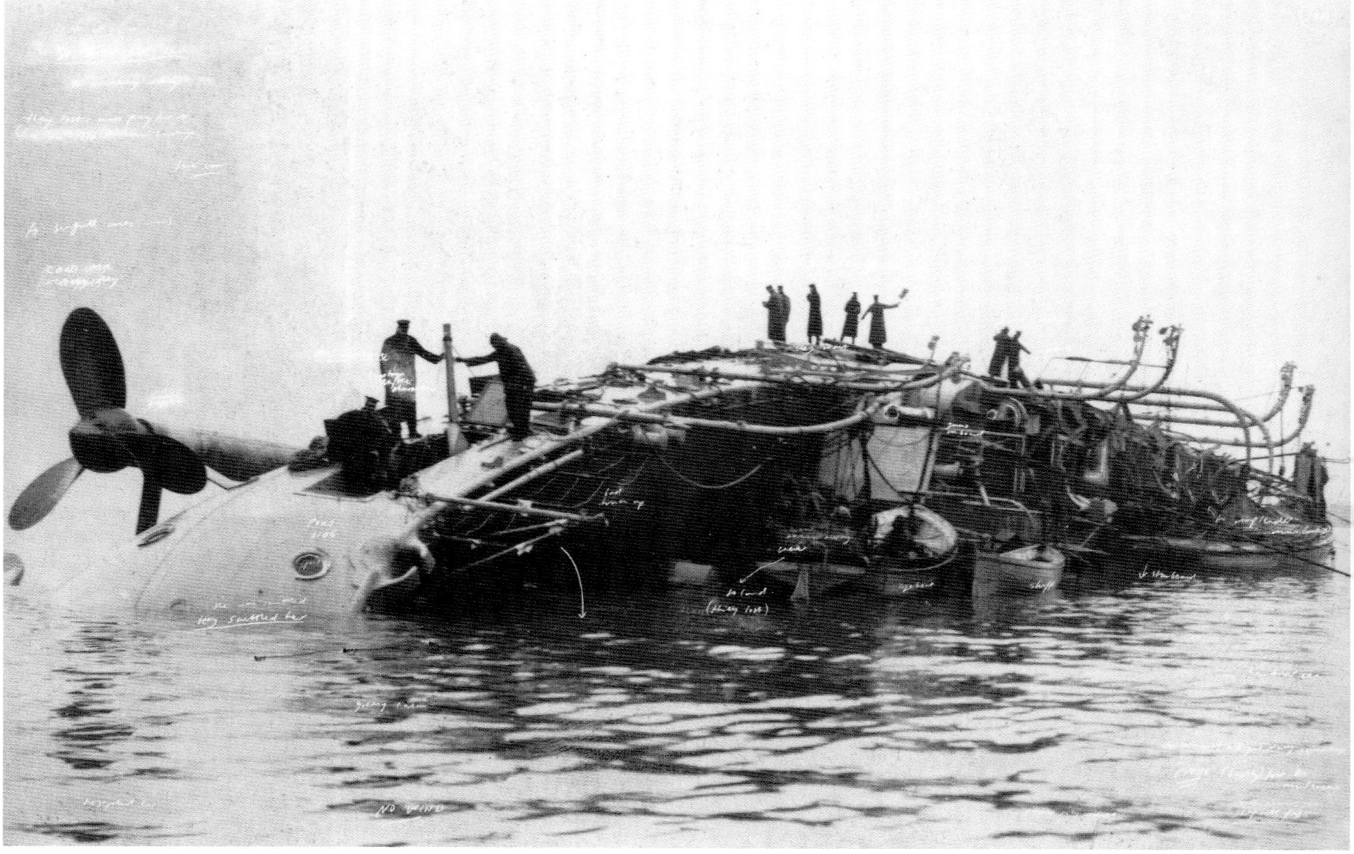

NO WIND 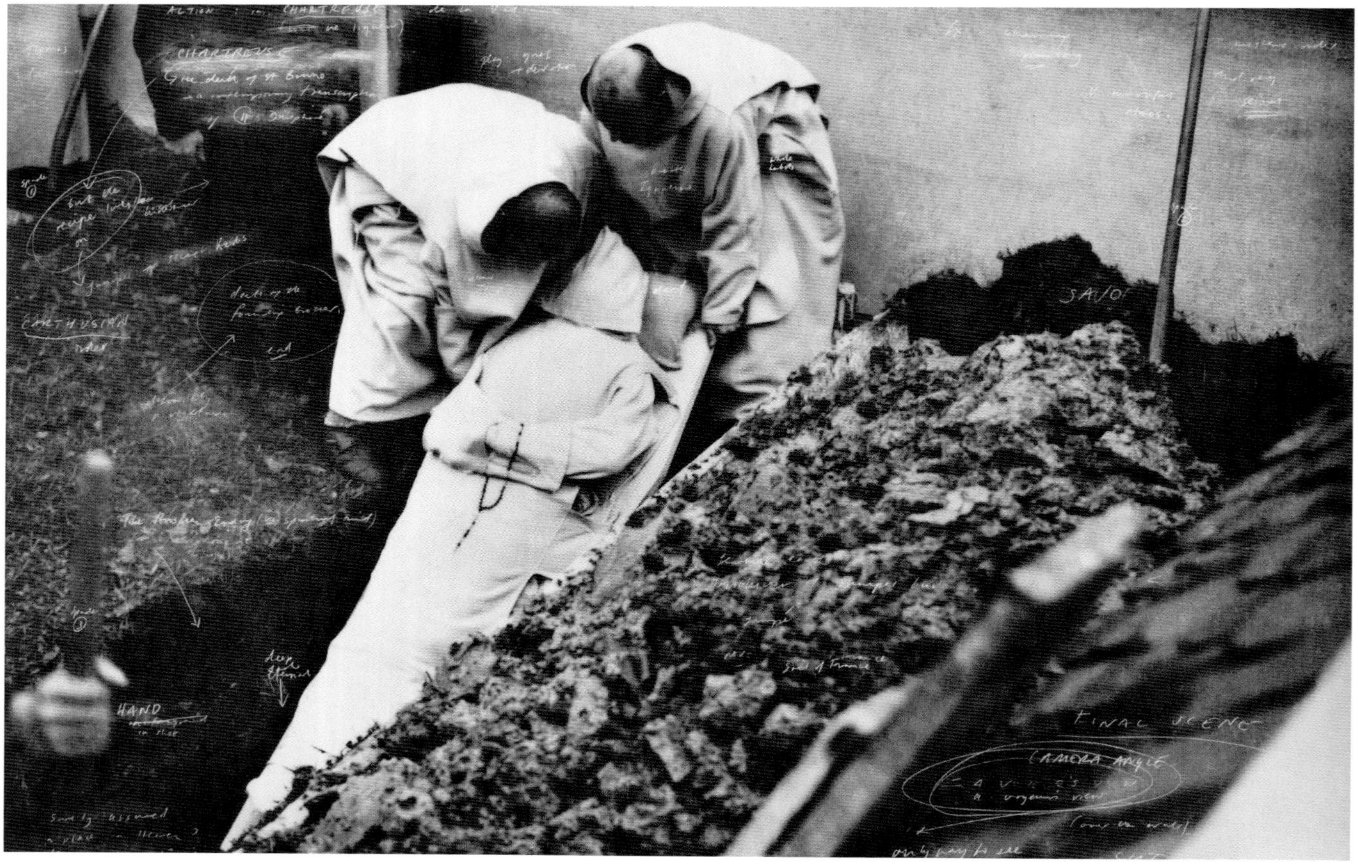
ACTION
CHARTREUSE
CHARTREUSE
The death of St Bruno
CARTHUSIAN
death of the founding brother
end
SAND
HAND
FINAL SCENE
CAMERA ANGLE
a voyeur's view

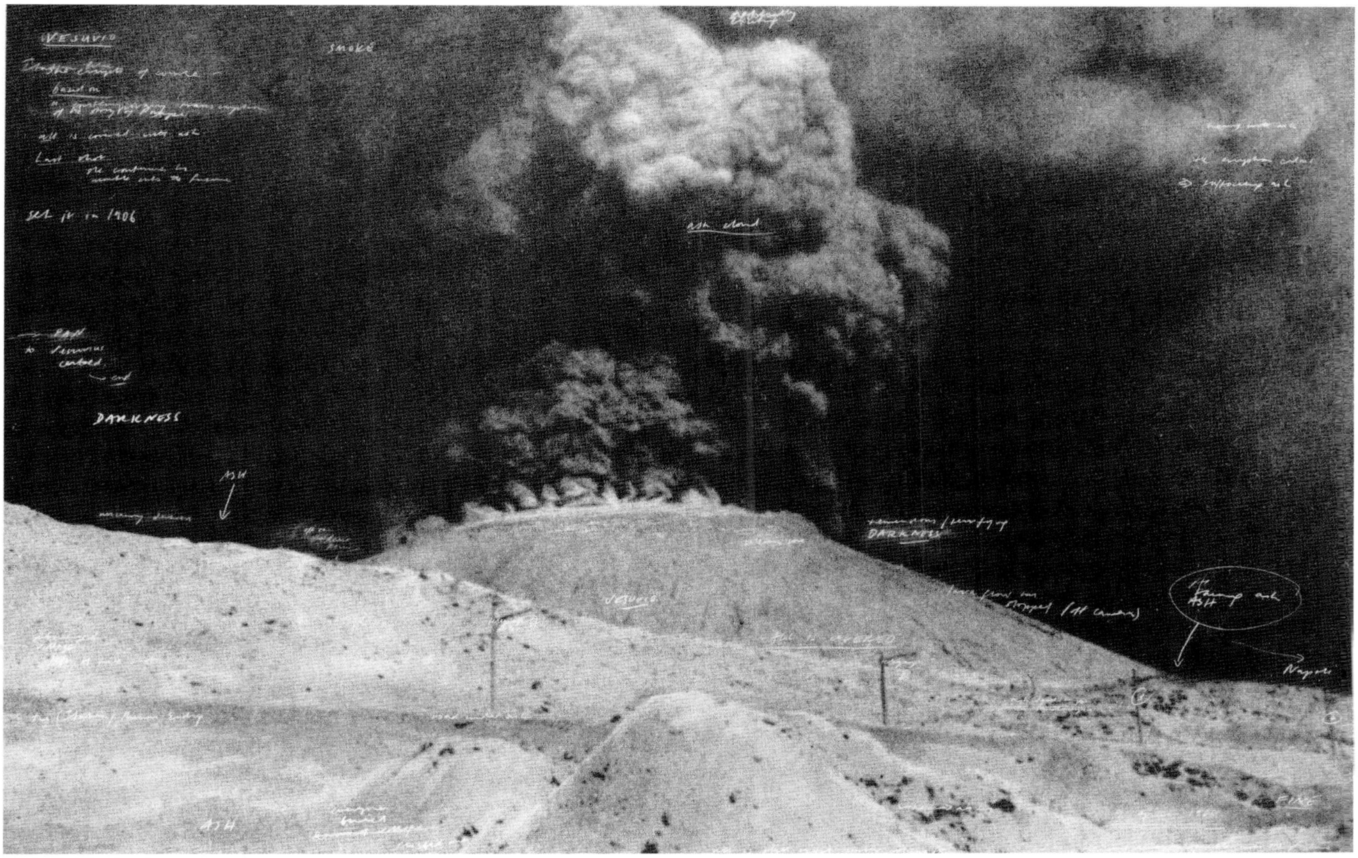

VESUVIO

SMOKE

set it in 1906

DARKNESS

ASH

DARKNESS

ASH

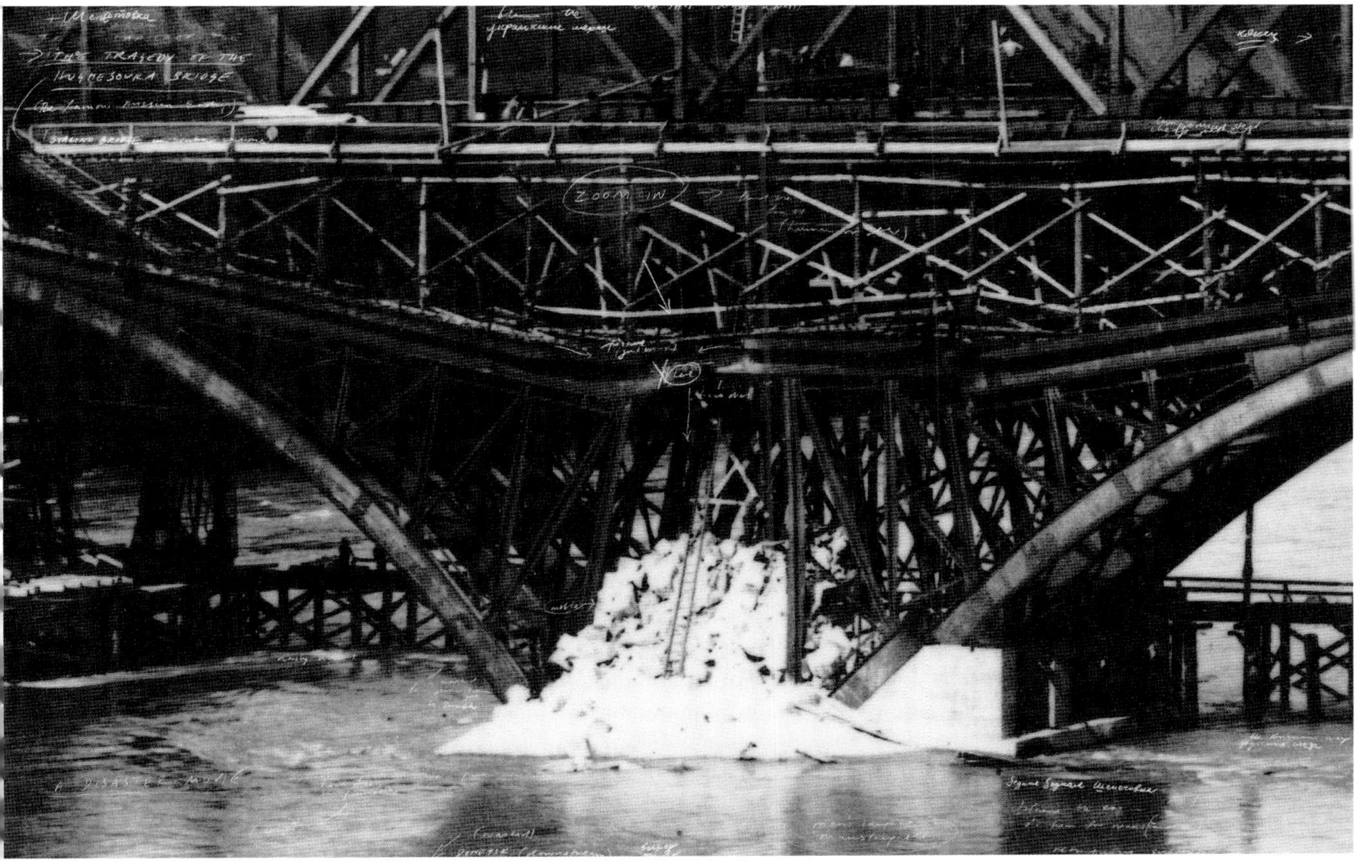

THE TRAGEDY OF THE ... BRIDGE

ZOOM IN

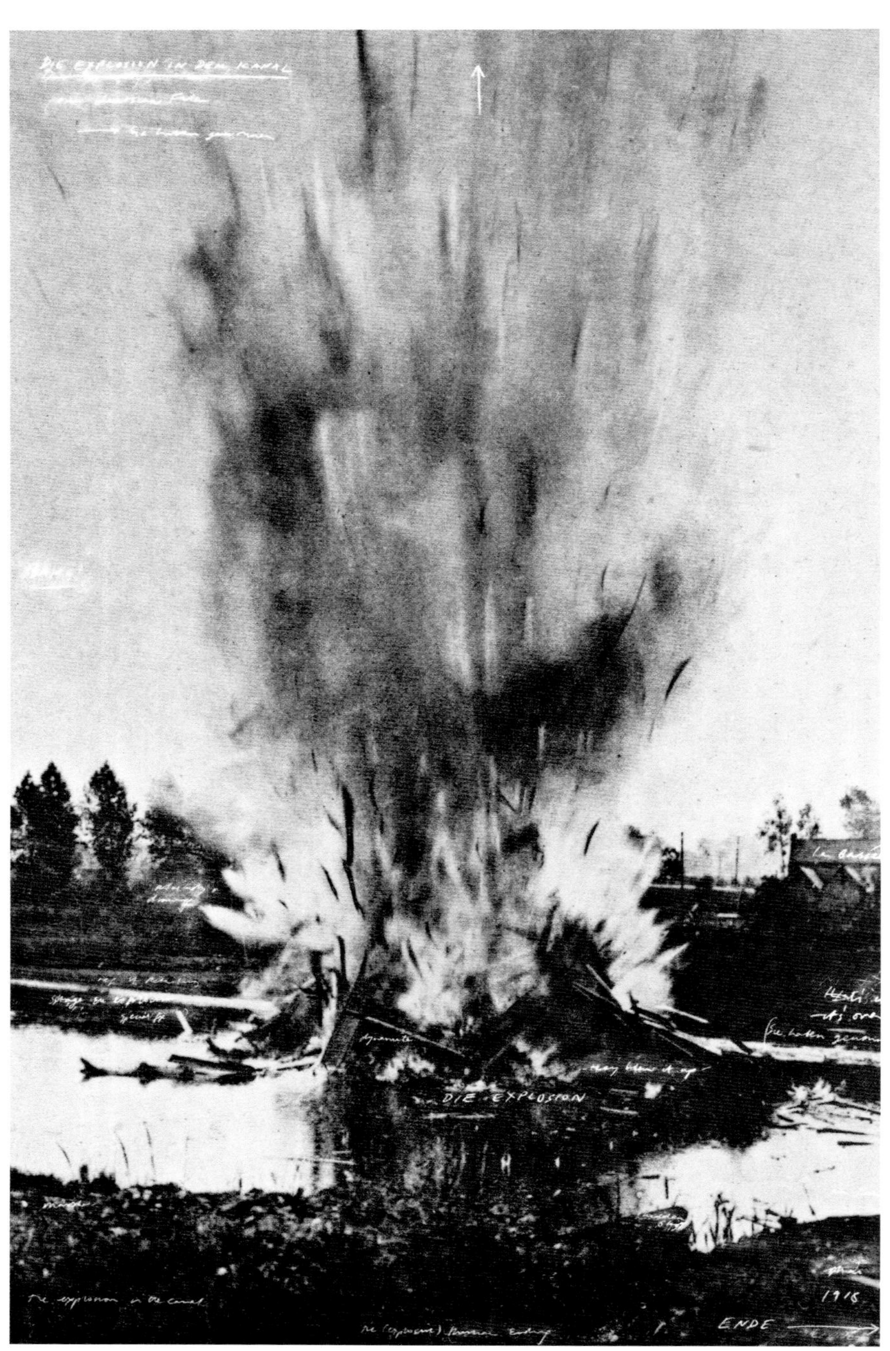
DIE EXPLOSION IN DEM KANAL
DIE EXPLOSION
ENDE
1918

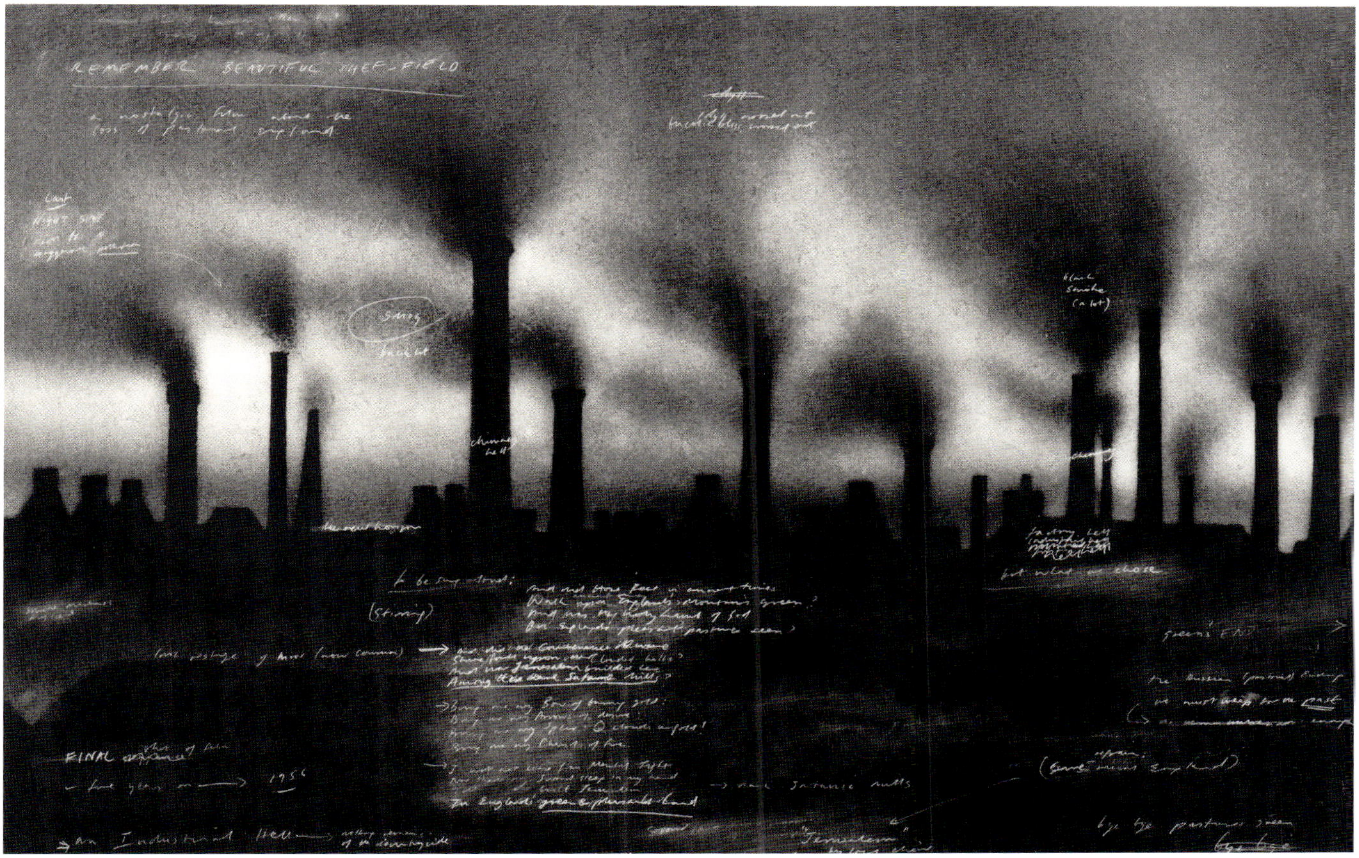

REMEMBER BEAUTIFUL SHEF-FIELD

→ an Industrial Hell

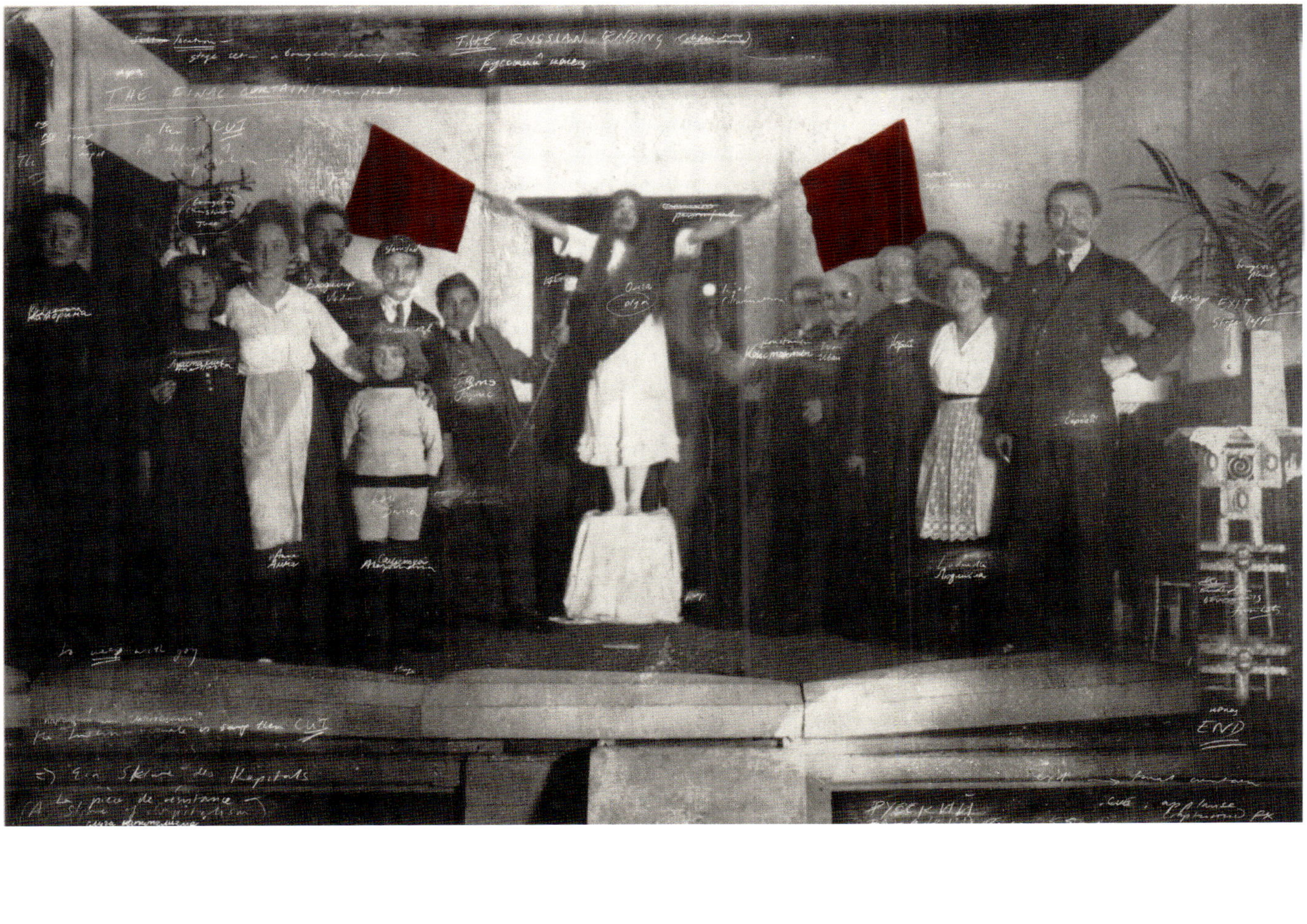

THE RUSSIAN ENDING

THE FINAL CURTAIN

END

Found Postcard Monoprints (Actors), 2018 (detail)
16 found postcards with printer ink
Each c. 8.6 x 13.7 cm

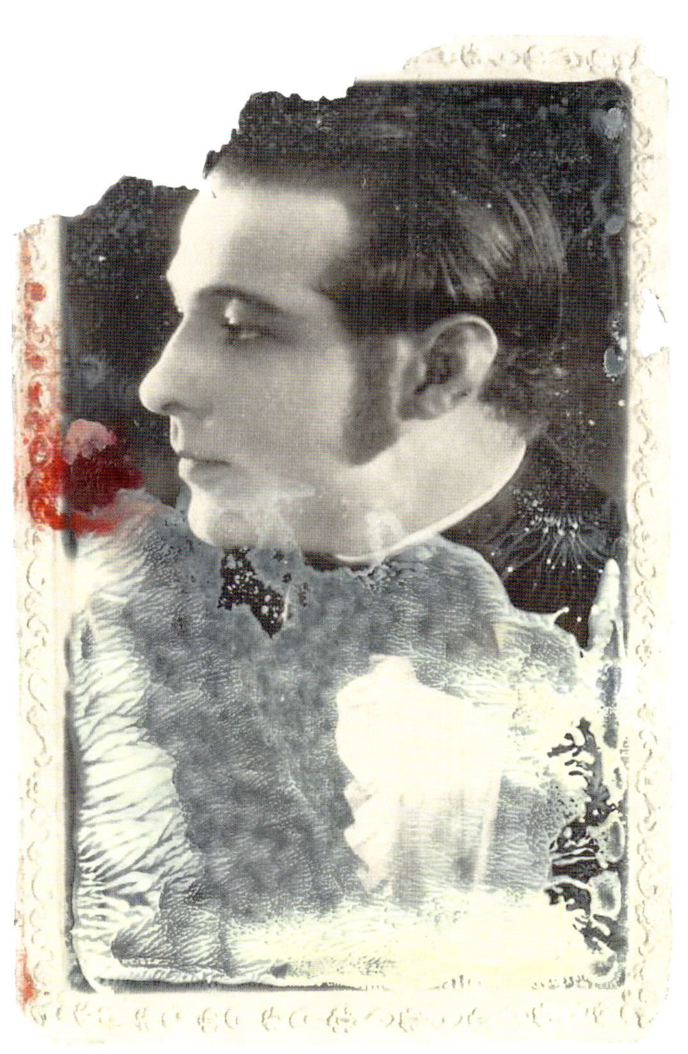

A Muse, 2017 (film stills)
35mm colour anamorphic film, optical sound,
reduced to spherical 16mm for exhibition,
2½ minutes

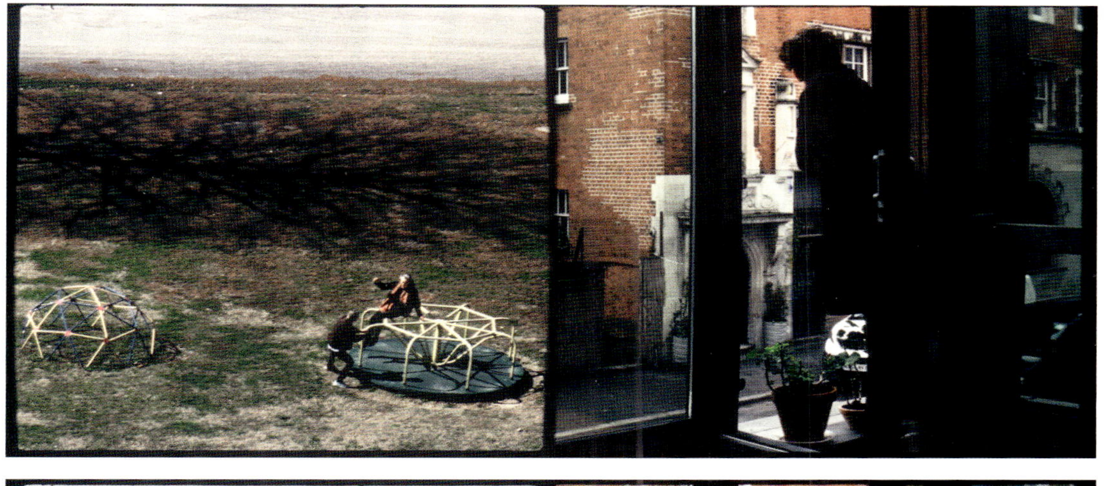

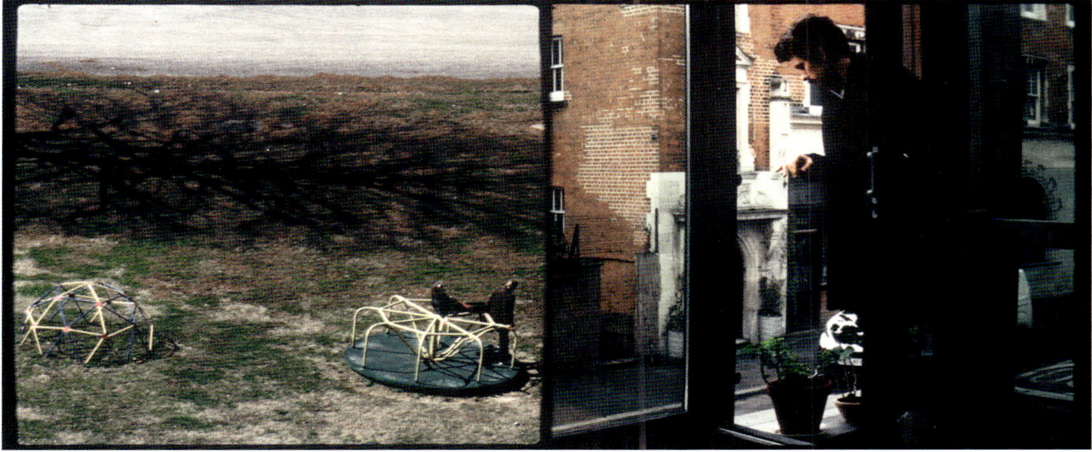

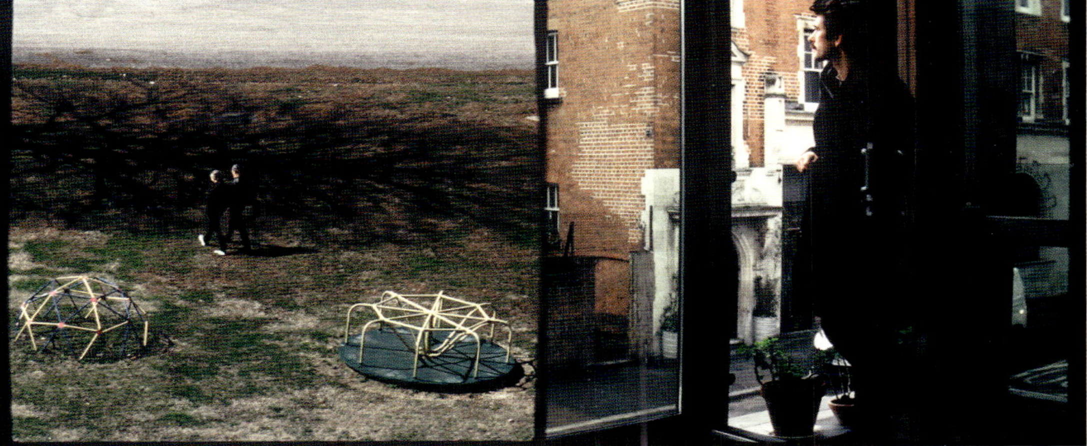

Tacita Dean in conversation with Hal Foster

Hal Foster It's a rich work, Tacita. We don't want to disenchant it too much, but I do have a few questions for you. Maybe you could begin with an account of your interaction with Stephen Dillane in the preparation of the text? For example, why the period wigs? What did you want to signal in terms of theatre?

Tacita Dean I was asked to make something for a stage, and for me that was a very simple equation – a stage meant acting. Clearly it can mean other things to other people, but I thought I'd like to work with an actor. I came from a position of total ignorance; I realised I knew next to nothing about acting or about theatre, so I began thinking of all the obvious tropes of theatre – theatricality, stage make-up, wigs, actor – and it evolved from that. It was an evolving thing, and retrospectively I can't tell you how miraculous certain decisions were; they came out of the process. It wasn't until we were rehearsing in Sydney that we decided to address what he should wear. So I had gone without any idea what he should look like, and because I had four performance nights that turned into a different theatrical wig each night. What had always fascinated me was stage fright: the idea of actors losing their way on stage. I thought that must be a terrible situation to be in. That was the premise behind the work: becoming conscious of oneself acting. Actually, I misunderstood so much about theatre. I have learnt a lot.

HF I want to ask about self-consciousness in a moment. But, first, what is the relationship between the memories the actor relates, which seem actual enough, and the texts he quotes, such as *The Tempest* and *On the Marionette Theatre*, which are all about artifice? You must have known you wanted to work with those two texts.

TD The process began with me talking to Stephen over a long period of time in London. We'd sit talking and *The Tempest* came up. Mathew [Hale] told me about *On the Marionette Theatre* – the Heinrich von Kleist text – and it evolved like that. Even the device of the chalk circle representing the inside and the outside was something we developed in Sydney. If you notice every time Stephen says something that sounds autobiographical, he steps outside of the circle, he even slips in and out at certain points. It wasn't a fixed thing at all; we had to work with it as a living thing.

HF And yet the result seems so seamless, even though it's all about showing the seams.

TD That's what I mean by miraculous.

HF So there really is magic in theatre?

TD Well, there is, yes, in a way but I'm thinking of the magic inside the process of making something: making the film, for example, and then using the four wigs

– a different wig for each of the four nights, and realising that I should cut across the four nights to make one performance and then appreciating more the significance of the different wigs. And it becoming about the joy of editing actually, and working with material, like being a sculptor, cutting it to make it work in that way. Even in the opening darkness, I edited all four wigs together; he's wearing all four wigs at that moment. Likewise with the 'this is not a great text' sequence, all the four wigs are in those moments. Also, of course, it gives you a clue – that I am cutting across the four performances – a clue that actually it wasn't spontaneous but scripted. A lot of people thought that he was 'doing it on the night', but then I wouldn't have been able to edit over four nights without the repetition of the performance. So in this way the film has a different identity to the actual performance because then you didn't know what was real and what was not, and whether he actually stormed out or not. Playing with the tension of that moment, for example, and keeping that within the film was quite important, holding that period of discomfort, even with film – how many people start thinking 'come on…'

HF 'Come on' what?

TD You know in that period when he's left the stage and people are thinking 'what's happening?' And I just hold a single shot, which is a very dull shot, to try to maintain the discomfort.

HF What do you say to him in that moment when he says, 'what?' That seems to be one moment of real rupture.

TD When I have my line? That one?

HF Yes.

TD He gave me that line.

HF He gave you that line at that very moment or in that text.

TD Well … that's the question. My line was, 'That must have been awful.'

HF In relation to that moment he's experiencing on the stage as rupture? Let me ask you about this trope of 'the membrane' you use, specifically in relation to theatre. You say you didn't know much about theatre…?

TD I knew about the fourth wall, but when you're in the round, which we were, surrounded by the audience on all sides, in a circle, it did feel that the metaphor of the membrane was more suitable somehow. A wall is something too rigid. Do you remember the semi-permeable membrane, which is the skin? There was something about the metaphor of the membrane that worked very well for that kind of more porous interaction.

HF Also, film can be seen as a membrane. The trope extends to your use of that medium too, making what we often take to be a fixed medium more flexible.

TD In 2014, when Juliana Engberg invited me to do something for the Sydney Biennial, she said, 'Well, you're losing your medium, why not try something else?' She was talking about the end of the medium of film, so she gave me the opportunity of working over four nights in a theatre. Four nights on a stage. Early on I wanted to bring in film precisely to show the fact that film runs out and that inevitably forces you into different views, which is why I had two cameras, one inside the circle and one outside. And the calling of the boards is an essential part of using film: the clapperboard is the way to mark a sync point simultaneously on the film and the sound, but having him call out the end boards was its own rupture device, breaking the artifice.

HF That's the main question here: the status of the artifice.

TD That is the main question, Hal. That *is* the main question.

HF We've arrived at the main question…

TD But it's difficult to talk about this work because I don't want to give it all away.

HF I don't want to know about the nuts and bolts, but I want to know about your relationship to this membrane and its rupture. If any of us have any avant-gardist blood in our veins still, we think that it should be ruptured, that's the Brechtian moment, we are for disenchantment, defamiliarisation, alienation even. And you raise that tradition in the text and in the performance, but you step aside from it too.

TD What's the difference between that and a deliberate rupture?

HF It seemed that the rupture caused by the exit sign and the woman with the red hat was a real rupture – real almost in the traumatic sense – and that almost no one wants.

TD Yes, but for him it was both.

HF It was both what?

TD It was both rupture and enchantment. It was both.

HF You mean he could recoup a real rupture as a moment of magic, and so somehow move from 'drying' to 'flying'?

TD Not exactly. Different moments but similar signifiers. It was a really profound thing, his description of 'drying'.

HF 'Drying' is what exactly? When you lose your lines?

TD Yes, stage fright, when you lose your lines. Actually, the deeper thing is that you lose faith in what you're doing. At that point you panic and you see the woman in the red hat and you see the fire exit signs – this is his point. But he says that when you're *in* it, in the zone, as it were, you can also see the woman in the red hat and the fire exits, but you're still 'flying', you're embodied. You're aware of it, but you can absorb it. He uses the word 'embody' quite a lot. Actors seem to use that word a lot; they embody a text. The importance of the text to an actor had evaded me, because, of course, an actor is only there at the agency of the text. So when he says: 'this is not a great text', he is basically saying 'you are going to screw me badly by putting me up there with this shit text.'

HF Is that where the Kleist trope of total self-consciousness or no self-consciousness at all comes in? The actor as God or puppet? Actually, at that moment, the actor is both.

TD Yes, well, that's the point. In the end, from what I can gather, they are indistinguishable at a certain point. But actually both states are quite rare, if you know what I mean.

HF So, to press a bit on the ideas of disenchantment and re-enchantment in the work…

TD Well, I think, that's the same thing.

HF The same thing or a relay between two things? My experience of *Event for a Stage* is this: you let more reality onto the stage, you force it through the membrane; at the same time you let more fiction out into the world, you force it through the membrane in the other direction. The moments of memory that he brings into play, they tend to be traumatic – the loss of his brother and his parents, the event on the highway in France – but somehow they don't effect a rupture because they become somewhat fictive in his telling. I guess that's also there in *The Tempest.* In the end you fall less on the side of Brecht and more on the side of – I don't know – Laurence Sterne?

TD Probably. I think I'm more for enchantment than for disenchantment.

HF 'To lay bare the device,' in this case, is to show the making of the film in the film – that move used to be on the side of disenchantment. But here it doesn't get us out into the real, so to speak; rather, it brings the real into your fictive world. It slips over to the side of re-enchantment.

TD Probably.

HF [Pause] We've never agreed like this before.

TD It's partly because I'm somebody who doesn't like to … I like to work on the level just below the conscious level. So what you're saying makes sense to me, but it's not something I would ever allow myself to go and pick over.

HF Because that would be to disenchant it somehow?

TD Yes. I don't want to disenchant everything, and it is a bit like that, and we're on very shaky ground here, because there's a hell of a lot I could tell you, and I don't want to tell you.

HF This is a conversation! There are people who want to know.

TD It is actually to do with exactly what you're saying, Hal: the level of enchantment I'm willing to keep to my chest. That's the area that *Event for a Stage* exists in. Yes, I lay bare the devices, but the devices, probably because they are theatrical, like the wigs and the make-up, are overdone. So I know what you're saying and I think you're right, but it was more about bringing the enchantment in, that way round – that's more me, for sure – than about bringing in things that *could* disenchant. I don't think they in any way *did* disenchant.

HF Again, I think it's both. On the one hand, you let the real into the fictive world, as with his apparent actual memories that become stories in the telling. On the other hand, you let the fictive into the real world, as when the actor leaves the stage – you know he'll come back, so that's not a rupture.

TD I agree. I don't think that is a rupture, actually. I knew that.

HF That's why I asked you what you said to him since that actually did seem to me to be a real rupture.

TD When he says, 'what?' and I say, 'that must have been awful'?

HF Right.

TD … awful to forget the lines of *The Tempest*? Actually I will give you this piece of information – he had to stay in that way until I said those words to him. The longer I didn't say them, the longer he had to hold that state.

HF Is that what he means about the space between texts? With a great text, he says, the actor is present, or confident in his presence, but he also uses this line (maybe it's your line) about 'the space between texts'. Care to unpack that one for us?

TD At that point, I think that just means, life, doesn't it?

HF I wouldn't know.

TD Isn't he saying that life is text, and an actor embodies various texts and then there's this time between texts? And I think an actor sometimes does struggle with the time between texts, because they need the text to…

HF In life, or on the stage? Or both?

TD Both.

HF What about the figure of the actor as a 'good parent'? That's a beautiful moment in your text.

TD It comes from *The Tempest.*

HF You mean you adapt the idea?

TD He is saying that, like a good parent, you have to protect your audience's belief while at the same time struggling to keep hold of your own belief.

HF A play between belief and trust. What about the distinction between self-consciousness and self-awareness?

TD I think that's the difference between flying and drying. I think when you're flying you're self-aware and when you're drying you are self-conscious. That's what I meant earlier – you suddenly become aware of your own artifice and everything falls apart. That's when you see everybody in the audience and you can't sustain the artifice anymore. But when you're in a state of euphoria and you're *flying*, to use that expression, you see everybody in the audience and you *can* sustain the artifice: you are aware of the situation; you are aware of being an actor on stage but it functions – the fourth wall is functioning. Whereas when you're self-conscious, it has completely fallen apart, the membrane has broken because you're no longer functioning with your own fourth wall, with your own membrane.

HF But I think you do more. I see that flying is a real high for an actor, but in this piece you expand the membrane. It's not just a nice ride *with* the membrane, you expand it; you open it up. It has to do with the permeability in the piece between performance art, theatre and film.

TD That's interesting, as at the start I had an idea of what I thought theatre was and Stephen had an idea of what he thought art was. And ne'er the twain do meet. So what we had to make was something else in a way, because we couldn't speak normally for a while.

HF One last question. There's this beautiful moment where he talks about his mother in the nursing home and how her friends have conversations and the threads of these conversations just disappear. And then towards the end he talks about how the actor assembles threads into a rope that he uses to hoist himself up. It's a beautiful notion, and I wondered how it came about.

TD It's how it all came about and I'm not going to tell you … It was an incredibly organic thing. It was actually like assembling a rope too. It kept evolving and became what it did. And so you're asking me, in a way, to understand how it came about, but I also almost don't know how it came about. It was really quite special.

Recorded at Metrograph in New York City on 4 November 2017.
Presented jointly by Marian Goodman Gallery and 601 Artspace.

This book is published on the occasion of the exhibition **Tacita Dean: Woman with a Red Hat**

7 July – 30 September 2018
The Fruitmarket Gallery, Edinburgh

List of works in the exhibition:

All works are by Tacita Dean. Courtesy the artist; Frith Street Gallery, London and Marian Goodman Gallery, New York/Paris unless otherwise stated. Measurements are given in centimetres, height x width.

A Muse, 2017
35mm colour anamorphic film, optical sound, reduced to spherical 16mm for exhibition, 2½ minutes.

With: Anne Carson, Robert Currie and Ben Whishaw; Director of Photography: Jamie Cairney; Focus Puller: Chris Connatty; Mask Technical Director: Cate Smierciak; Mask Supervisor: Cleo Walker; Location Sound Recordists: Steve Felton (UK) and Nick Campbell (US); Loaders: Clare Connor (UK) and Ian McAvoy (US); Grip: Alex Webb Allen; Driver: Mark Crane (UK); Aperture Gate Masks Concept: © Michael Bölling/Barkow Leibinger Architects/Tacita Dean, Berlin; *A Muse* Masks Design: Michael Bölling; Mask Production Berlin: Cleo Walker and Annette Ueberlein; Mask Printing: Fastpart Kunstofftechnik GmbH; Production UK: Pinky Ghundale; Production US: Noorhayati Said, Marine Pariente; Production Assistants: Ida Champion, Jessica Simas; Second unit US: Jimmy Fahey, Alexander Hahn, Paul Ruffolo, Brad Smith, Becky Werve; Marketing Executive Panavision Hollywood: Jennifer Kuwabara Naples; Specialist Lens Expertise: Guy McVicker; Lens Technician Lead: Ye Woo Kim; Sound Design: James Harrison; Sound Logistics: Steve Felton, The Sound Design Company; Exposed Negative Transport: Reels on Wheels; Neg Cut: Mo Henry; Rushes: FotoKem, Los Angeles; Film Scheduler: Denise Marques; Optical reduction: Vince Roth and Frank Escobar; Colour Timing: Doug Ledin; Printed by: FotoKem, Los Angeles; Filmed using: Panavision® Camera and Lenses; Installation: Kenneth Graham, KS Objectiv; Originated on: Kodak Motion Picture Film; Very special thanks: Anne Carson, Robert Currie and Ben Whishaw; With thanks: Jeff Clarke, Steven Overman, Sam Clarke and Beverly Pasterczyk, Kodak; Debbie McNelly Goins and Thebes Historical Society; Made with financial assistance from Frith Street Gallery, London with thanks to Jane Hamlyn and Dale McFarland, and Marian Goodman Gallery, New York/Paris with thanks to Marian Goodman, Rose Lord and Marine Pariente

Filmed on location in London and Thebes, Illinois

Event for a Stage, 2014
Gouache on found postcard, used for the poster for *Event for a Stage*, Carriageworks, May 2014
8.6 x 13.7 cm

Event for a Stage, 2015
16mm colour film, optical sound
50 minutes

Actor: Stephen Dillane; Director of Photography: Jamie Cairney; Camera Operator: Tom Wright; Focus Puller: Chris Connatty and Cate Smierciak; Lighting Designer: Nicholas Rayment; Sound Designer: Hayley Forward; Film Technical Assistant: Emma Sullivan; Assistant: Cleo Walker; Artistic Director: Juliana Engberg; Performance Curator: Rosie Fisher; Production Manager: Josh Green; ABC RN Audio Technician: Mark Don; Stage Manager: Samantha Morrison; Make up and Wigs: Dennis Adolphe; Wigs and Dressing: Opera Australia, Lyn Heal and Stefanie Paglialonga; Equipment hire: Panavision, Paul Jackson and Brian Flexmore; Gear Head; Norwest Productions; Rushes: Neglab, Sydney; DeJonghe Film Postproduction, Kortrijk; Editor: Tacita Dean; Sound Editor: James Harrison; Neg Cut: Steve Farman; Printed by: FotoKem, Los Angeles; Installation: Kenneth Graham, KS Objectiv; Originated on: Kodak Motion Picture Film; Co-commissioned by: Carriageworks and the 19th Biennale of Sydney in Association with ABC RN; With additional support of: Frith Street Gallery, London and Marian Goodman Gallery, New York/Paris; With thanks: Katie Mitchell; Thomas Oberender; Juliana Engberg; Lisa Havilah; Marah Braye; Gina Hall; Talia Linz; Anita Tscherne; Thomas Demand; Jennifer Kuwabara; Samuel Hodge; Zan Wimberley; Werner Winkelmann; Michelle Healey/Carcanet Press; Jane Hamlyn, Dale McFarland, Marian Goodman and Rose Lord; Mathew Hale and Rufus Hale

Written in collaboration with Stephen Dillane. Reading from *On the Marionette Theatre*, Heinrich von Kleist, 1810. Adapted from a translation by Idris Parry in *Hand to Mouth and Other Essays*, Carcanet Press, 1981. Original performances filmed between 1–4 May 2014 at Carriageworks, Sydney

Foley Artist, 1996
Laserdisc and monitor, 8 speakers, Akai DD8 playback machine, Sondor magnetic playback machine, dubbing chart lightbox
Tate: Purchased 2002

Actor: Tim Pigott-Smith; Foley Artists: Stan Fiferman, Beryl Mortimer; Camera: John Adderley; Clapper: Pip Laurenson; Sound Editor: Martin Cantwell; Technical Advisor; Mike Dowson; Production Supervisor: Steve Felton; Editor: Rob Wright; Sound Post Production: The Sound Design Company; Stills Photographer: Stephen White; Online: Evolution Televison Ltd; Installation: Kenneth Graham, KS Objectiv; Made for *Art Now*, Tate Gallery, London

Videoed on location at Delta Sound, Shepperton Studios.

Found Postcard Monoprints (Actors), 2018

16 found postcards with printer ink
Each c. 8.6 x 13.7 cm

His Picture in Little, 2017
35mm colour anamorphic film, silent, reduced to spherical 16mm for exhibition as a miniature, 15½ minutes, continuous loop

With: Stephen Dillane, David Warner and Ben Whishaw; Director of Photography: Jamie Cairney; Focus Puller: Chris Connatty; Mask Technical Director: Cate Smierciak; Mask Supervisor: Cleo Walker; Loaders: Clare Connor, Clare Fuller (UK) and Ian McAvoy (US); Grip: Alex Webb Allen; Driver (UK): Mark Crane; Aperture Gate Masks Concept: © Michael Bölling/Barkow Leibinger Architects/Tacita Dean, Berlin; *His Picture in Little* Masks Design: Michael Bölling; Mask Production Berlin: Cleo Walker and Annette Ueberlein; Mask Printing: Fastpart Kunstofftechnik GmbH; Production (UK): Pinky Ghundale; Production (US): Noorhayati Said, Marine Pariente; Production Manager (UK): Kelly Taylor; Production Assistants: Ida Champion, Jessica Simas; Location Manager (UK): Emma Griffiths; Catering: Farmhouse Catering, Bodmin; Second unit (US): Jimmy Fahey, Alexander Hahn, Paul Ruffolo, Brad Smith, Becky Werve; Marketing Executive Panavision Hollywood: Jennifer Kuwabara Naples; Specialist Lens Expertise: Guy McVicker; Lens Technician Lead: Ye Woo Kim; Exposed Negative Transport: Reels on Wheels; Neg Cut: Mo Henry; Rushes: Cinelab, London and FotoKem, Los Angeles; Film Scheduler: Denise Marques; Optical reduction: Vince Roth and Frank Escobar; Colour Timing: Doug Ledin; Printed by: FotoKem, Los Angeles; Filmed using: Panavision® Camera and Lenses; Installation: Kenneth Graham, KS Objectiv; Originated on: Kodak Motion Picture Film; Very special thanks: Stephen Dillane, David Warner and Ben Whishaw; With thanks to: Tom Tykwer, Katie Mitchell and Julian Belfrage Associates; Steve Felton, Andy Paddon and Nick Campbell, David Luck; Trethevy Barton Farm; Krysia Osostowicz of Lavethan House; Julie Throssell and Colin Greenaway of Ivey; Jonny Bamford; Martin Press of Malplaquet House, Nicholas Cullinan, Tim Knox; Sarah Lea. And thanks to: Jeff Clarke, Steven Overman, Sam Clarke and Beverly Pasterczyk, Kodak; Adrian Bull, Cinelab; Derek Gillbard, Eliot House Hotel, Liskeard; Made with financial assistance from Frith Street Gallery, London with thanks to Jane Hamlyn and Dale McFarland, and Marian Goodman Gallery, New York/Paris with thanks to Marian Goodman, Rose Lord and Marine Pariente

Filmed on location in London, Bodmin Moor and Thebes, Illinois.

Providence, 2017
35mm colour anamorphic film, silent, reduced to spherical 16mm for exhibition, 5½ minutes, continuous loop

With: David Warner; Directors of Photography: Jamie Cairney (UK) and Travis LaBella (US); Focus Pullers: Chris Connatty (UK), Gary Webster (US); Mask Technical Director: Cate Smierciak; Mask Supervisor: Cleo Walker (UK); Second AC: Cody Banks (US); Loaders: Clare Fuller (UK) and Craig Samuels (US); Grip: Alex Webb Allen (UK); Driver: Mark Crane (UK); Aperture Gate Masks Concept: © Michael Bölling/Barkow Leibinger; Architects/Tacita Dean, Berlin; *Providence* Masks Design: Michael Bölling; Mask Production Berlin: Cleo Walker and Annette Ueberlein; Mask Printing: Fastpart Kunstofftechnik GmbH; Production UK: Pinky Ghundale; Production US: Noorhayati Said, Marine Pariente; Logistics Manager (Huntington Botanical Gardens): Rani Singh; Location Liaison (Huntington Botanical Gardens): Danielle Rudeen, John Trager; Production Assistants: Ida Champion, Jessica Simas; Marketing Executive Panavision Hollywood: Jennifer Kuwabara Naples; Specialist Lens Expertise: Guy McVicker; Lens Technician Lead: Ye Woo Kim; Exposed Negative Transport: Reels on Wheels; Exposed Negative Storage: The Academy Film Archive, Los Angeles with thanks to Mark Toscano; Neg Cut: Mo Henry; Rushes: Cinelab, London and FotoKem, Los Angeles; Film Scheduler: Denise Marques; Optical reduction: Vince Roth and Frank Escobar; Colour Timing Doug Ledin; Printed by: FotoKem, Los Angeles; Filmed using: Panavision® Camera and Lenses; Installation: Kenneth Graham, KS Objectiv; Originated on: Kodak Motion Picture Film; Very special thanks: David Warner; With thanks: Julian Belfrage Associates; Kevin Salatino, Huntington Botanical Gardens; Steve Felton, Andy Paddon, Martin Press of Malplaquet House, Nicholas Cullinan, Tim Knox; Additional thanks: Jeff Clarke, Steven Overman, Sam Clarke and Beverly Pasterczyk, Kodak; Adrian Bull, Cinelab; Made with financial assistance from Frith Street Gallery, London with thanks to Jane Hamlyn and Dale McFarland, and Marian Goodman Gallery, New York/Paris with thanks to Marian Goodman, Rose Lord and Marine Pariente

Filmed on location in London and Pasadena, California.

The Russian Ending, 2001
Portfolio of 20 photogravures on Hahnemühle Bütten 300g paper
Each 54 x 79.4 cm
Printed by Merete Helerøe, Mikkel Thieleman and Niels Borch Jensen, Copenhagen.
Published by Peter Blum, New York
Tate: Presented by the artist 2002

When first I raised the Tempest, 2016
Chalk on blackboard
244 x 976 cm
Glenstone Museum, Potomac, Maryland

The Fruitmarket Gallery extends our sincere thanks to the lenders to the exhibition, Glenstone and Tate, and to Maria Gabriela Mizes and Steven O'Banion at Glenstone, and Maria Balshaw, Ann Gallagher and Louisa Joseph at Tate who have made the loans possible. Our thanks also to Tacita Dean and Hal Foster for permission to publish the text of their public conversation at Metrograph, New York and to Martyn Ridgewell for his assistance with this publication. We are grateful also to Cleo Walker and all at the studio of Tacita Dean, and to Ken Graham of KS Objectiv for his technical expertise and advice. Thanks also to Jane Hamlyn and all at Frith Street Gallery, London, especially Dale McFarland, and to Marian Goodman, Rose Lord and Marine Pariente at Marian Goodman Gallery, New York. And finally, our especial thanks to Tacita Dean for the enthusiasm, energy and commitment that she has brought to the planning of this exhibition and publication, and for making it possible to share her wonderful work with our audiences.

Tacita Dean thanks Stephen Dillane, and David Warner, Ben Whishaw, Anne Carson & Robert Currie, Tim Pigott-Smith, Stan Fiferman and Beryl Mortimer for appearing in these works and also the great film (and video) crews she has worked with over the years to make them. She thanks Sidney Felsen & Joni Weyl Felsen of Gemini G.E.L for accommodating so generously the making of the monoprints; she warmly thanks Hal Foster, Martyn Ridgewell, Ken Graham, Frank Müller and her studio: Cleo Walker, Eva Eicker and Christina Haufe. She thanks everyone at The Fruitmarket Gallery, her galleries Frith Street Gallery, London and Marian Goodman Gallery, New York/Paris, and Mathew & Rufus Hale

Tacita Dean: Woman with a Red Hat

Published by The Fruitmarket Gallery
45 Market Street, Edinburgh, EH1 1DF
Tel: +44 (0)131 225 2383
www.fruitmarket.co.uk

Edited by Fiona Bradley
Designed and typeset by Elizabeth McLean
Assisted by Susan Gladwin

Distributed by Art Data
12 Bell Industrial Estate,
50 Cunnington Street, London W4 5HB
Tel: +44 (0)208 747 1061
www.artdata.co.uk

ISBN 978-1-908612-52-6

All works illustrated are by Tacita Dean. Courtesy the artist; Frith Street Gallery, London and Marian Goodman Gallery, New York/Paris unless otherwise stated.

Photography credits: Zan Wimberley pp. 2–3, 9, 12; Steve White p. 4; Cathy Carver pp. 17–19; Fredrik Nilsen pp. 23–26; *Foley Artist*, 1996, Tacita Dean © Tate, London 2018 pp. 32–33

The Fruitmarket Gallery is a company limited by guarantee, registered in Scotland No. 87888 and registered as a Scottish Charity No. SC 005576. VAT No. 398 2504 21. Registered Office: 45 Market Street, Edinburgh, EH1 1DF

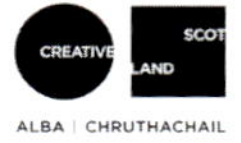